HOUSE STORY

Insider Secrets to the
Perfect Home Renovation

JASMINE ROTH

and Kelli Kehler

PHOTOGRAPHS BY DABITO

TEN SPEED PRESS
California | New York

CONTENTS

Introduction   1

1 | CREATING YOUR HOUSE STORY
7

2 | CURB APPEAL—IT'S WHAT'S
ON THE OUTSIDE THAT COUNTS
39

3 | KNOCKING DOWN WALLS—
THE LAYOUT LOWDOWN
65

4 | WALL TREATMENTS AND FLOOR
FINISHES—THE FOUNDATION
OF YOUR HOUSE STORY
81

5 | EVERYTHING KITCHEN—
THE HEART OF THE HOME
109

6 | IT'S NOT JUST A BATHROOM—
LOOKING AT THE LOO
153

7 | FIREPLACES, BOOKCASES,
AND HIDDEN SPACES
189

8 | PERSONALIZE AND DIYS—
TELLING YOUR HOUSE STORY
217

Appendix A: The Ultimate Jazzy's Picks—Three Home Designs   258
Appendix B: The Everything Kitchen Checklist   268
Appendix C: The Everything Bathroom Checklist   269
Appendix D: Quick Reference Toolbox—Jazzy's Favorites   270
Appendix E: Resources   274
Acknowledgments   277

INTRODUCTION

Have you ever walked into someone's home and realized it has nothing to say? We all have that friend with a larger-than-life personality—or maybe your friend is known as the super Zen, go-with-the-flow yoga enthusiast. You'd expect to walk into their homes and *feel* that personality come through, right? Well, you'd be surprised by just how many homes I've seen that had absolutely nothing to say about the unique people who live there.

Your house is the one place in this world that can be inherently, unapologetically *you*. Someone who has never met you should be able to walk into your house and immediately know who you are and what you're about. I believe that homes can talk—they can tell a story. They can tell us to relax, to be confident, and to live our lives with intention and integrity if we build them to be places that speak directly from our personality and serve our needs. I believe in surrounding ourselves with inspiration and living in a way that displays unquestionable purpose.

The decisions we make about our home's design and functionality form the foundation of our house story. Whether you're renting one room in an apartment or launching a full-blown home construction project, you can tell your house story so that where you live represents you and inspires you every day. And I truly believe that I'm the person to help you tackle this because of how I learned on the job. I've failed before so you don't have to.

You see, I didn't go to design school. I didn't go to contractor school. But fast forward a decade, I've built and designed hundreds of homes and have multiple seasons of my own HGTV home renovation show under my belt. I haven't been formally trained in any of the things I now do on a daily basis in my full-time job. I love building homes and I've had to learn as I go. I'm writing this today as a professional in the home renovation biz, but it wasn't that long ago that I was exactly where you are: embarking on a home renovation project and in way over my head.

In 2010, my husband, Brett, and I were building our first home together, and we had no idea what we were doing. We naively thought we'd joyfully pick paint colors together like they do on HGTV, say "That's the one!" and go have dinner. Boy, were we wrong. We thought our first home construction project was going to be so much easier than it actually was, and we didn't have the time, expertise, or knowledge to guide our project. We didn't know any of the things our contractor was asking of us, and it cost us money. Choosing the right paint color was the least of our concerns. After two years of drowning in our project, it became clear it was never going to get done unless one of us was there full-time. I gave notice at my corporate job, and the next thing I knew, I was on that job site every day, asking our contractor questions. I wanted to know how everything worked, to solve real home problems, and that was the beginning of my career. Obviously, not everyone is going to quit their job and fall into their future career. But because I went from literally not caring at all about design and construction to making it my profession and passion—in 0 to 60 speed—I have a unique perspective on how home renovations work.

What I'm saying to you is, *I've been there*. I get it. And because I'm not from any design school, I'm not beholden to any rigid design rules. I don't get caught up in whatever the latest fad or the hottest ticket item of the moment is—that's not what my clients need. What they need is a house that they can live in. And that's what I'm after here: I want your home to be livable, functional, beautiful, and incredibly personal. I want you to be comfortable in your home.

So, if it's midnight, and you're sitting on your kitchen floor surrounded by paint swatches and hardware samples and you're pulling out your hair over all the decisions and uncertainty, take a deep breath and open up this book. *This* is the book I needed when I was where you are today, sitting on that kitchen floor in a crumpled heap of stress. I'm going to help you.

You've got this—now let's get started!

How to Use This Book

There are lots of helping hands throughout this book to guide you through your home project. Often the hardest and most confusing part of a home renovation project is knowing where to start and what your first step is. I've written this book to help you make use of my tips and tricks through your own personal lens (your house story) and gauge your project challenges upfront.

I'm kicking off with a chapter on creating your own story and explaining what the heck that means. I'm going to help you stick to this throughout your whole project, and your home will feel undeniably cohesive and unquestionably *YOU* as a result.

Every chapter will end with a Jazzy's Chapter Checklist, which is my version of "do not pass Go, do not collect $200." Because if you can't answer "yes" to all three questions in each chapter checklist, I'll have you go back and do some more work before we move on. We're going to take each step together to ensure your project goes off without a hitch.

I'm also giving out a TON of Pro Tips and coveted design secrets in each chapter. And keep an eye out for boxes titled Jazzy's Favorites, as well as helpful sidebars for goodies such as my most trusted paint colors, favorite hardware, and the best places to buy materials and products. I'll also cover questions to ask your contractor or what to say to the pros. All of these tips will be sprinkled throughout each chapter as a sort of "pull over, let me help you get to your destination" feature. I've also created worksheets to help you assess your space and figure out what you need to address for your own project. They might help you find something you would've totally overlooked!

And last but not least, I always start every one of my projects with a super-rad mood board to put all my ideas and choices into one place. Doing this really helps my clients envision the space and see the plan for what it's going to look like in the end. You'll find these mood boards throughout the book to help you get a sense of what I'm talking about. And if you're looking for some serious assistance in a "just tell me what to buy!" kind of way, I'm offering up three different home designs in an appendix of this book. Then you can just plug and play without any of the headaches! 🙂

You're not alone in this project, and you can totally do this. I believe in you, and I'm going to be there the whole time cheering you on!

Jasmine

1 CREATING YOUR HOUSE STORY

"Your house is the one place in this world that can be inherently, unapologetically *you*."

THE ROTHS
Established 2012

We all have a house story—we just need to write it! Why do you need to identify your house story, or style, for your home, both exterior and interior, you ask? Because it will guide every single decision you make in your home's design from the front door to the bathroom, and it will be a trusted companion to fall back on when you're stumped! Your house story identifies who you are and communicates your personal style.

And just so you know, the term "house story" is an easy catchphrase that you will refer to as you embark on your design journey. For example, I live in California. I like Cape Cod architecture because I went to college in Boston, and my husband and I always liked traveling to the beach in Massachusetts. The more gray wood shutters and intricate wood moldings there are, the better for me! My dream is to live in an industrial loft, but my property is close to the beach. My house story is a Traditional Cape Cod with Industrial accents. And, oh yeah, that's the first house I ever built.

This chapter will guide your entire project and be your roadmap throughout your renovation process—whether you're doing major construction on a home you own or you're making smaller cosmetic updates to a rental. Your house story is so much deeper than decor. If you have the opportunity to renovate, change, or build your house (the way you really want it), this is your chance to get your foot in the door with your own story. That way, at the end of the project, when the dust settles and you get to add in your decor, it will all layer together perfectly. These layers are what will make your design feel cohesive and finished.

Understanding your house story will also inform your discussions with your general contractor (GC) because you'll know how to communicate your wants and your vision. It'll give you the confidence to talk to your GC and other experts like a pro. So, no matter your living circumstance, your own story is essential and will help tell us exactly who you are. I've created a step-by-step process to figure this out, and it's painless . . . I promise!

Core Designs

Let's get to it, shall we? There are four core designs and one of these will be the base of your house story. They are **Contemporary**, **Cottage**, **Traditional**, and **Rustic**. (Going back to my example, Traditional is mine.) The core design is the guiding design for both your home's exterior and interior. And identifying which of these designs appeals most to you will help you to hone in on more specific elements of design that you're drawn to. Keep in mind that we're less focused on the historical and technical architectural definition of these styles and more focused on the design vibes associated with these terms today.

In most cases, your core design will be your home's current architectural style. This is a major part of your home that you probably won't change. Don't worry, though, we'll pair what's already there with other style add-ons. We'll get to those in a minute. Right now, we're picking the basics—the jeans and classic white T-shirt of your design—the core design. Or if you like to think in food terms, the first time I explained this to Brett, he was like, "Oh, so it's like building your own cheeseburger, right? The core design is the type of meat [I'm veggie or turkey, how 'bout you?] and then the style add-ons are all the toppings and well . . . add-ons." Leave it to Brett to break down my entire book into a cheeseburger analogy—ha!

If you're reading this and thinking "Come on, Jasmine! I have a sleek, modern home but I'm going to ignore that and make it feel all cottage-y on the inside. I dream of living in a cottage!" I'm going to stop you right there. There *is* a way to have both—your home *can* feel just like what you've always dreamed it would be, while also feeling like it makes sense. So, unless you're building a new home from the ground up (oh, you lucky duck!), the way we do that is by blending what you have to work with now with what you wish your home would look like. Let's explore these four core designs to figure out which one best describes your current home. If you're starting from the ground up, pick any core design your little heart desires.

CONTEMPORARY ORGANIC MIDMODERN

EXTERIOR

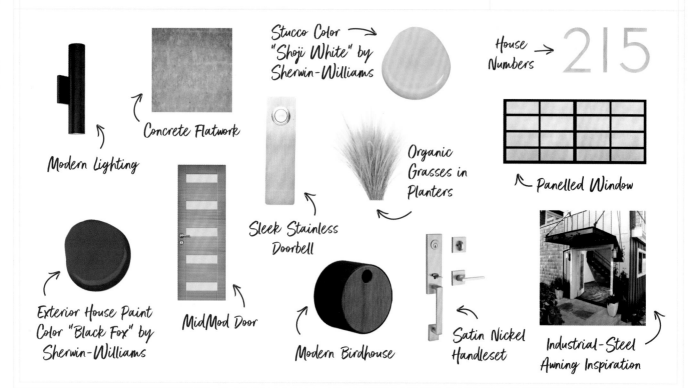

Modern Lighting

Concrete Flatwork

Stucco Color "Shoji White" by Sherwin-Williams

House Numbers → 215

Organic Grasses in Planters

Panelled Window

Exterior House Paint Color "Black Fox" by Sherwin-Williams

MidMod Door

Sleek Stainless Doorbell

Modern Birdhouse

Satin Nickel Handleset

Industrial-Steel Awning Inspiration

CONTEMPORARY ORGANIC MIDMODERN

BASICS

Wall Sconces Over Art

Custom Barn Door

Gray Roller Shades

Smoked-Wood Floors

Simple-Shaker Style Doors

Brass Cabinet Hardware

Wall-Mounted Toilets

Interior Wall Color "Pediment" by Sherwin-Williams

Lever Door Hardware

Contemporary

Homes that are Contemporary in style lean more modern and showcase clean lines, whether that's shown in furniture choices or architectural elements. Less is more when it comes to detail, and more simplistic materials are used in the design. If your home is already Midcentury Modern, or Industrial, or even Scandinavian in structure, this is your core design.

Cottage

Cottage style is all about charm and comfort. Weathered finishes are seen throughout, and texture is huge—the more cozy blankets, linen curtains, and beadboard siding there is, the better. On the exterior, this might mean a single-story house with smaller-scale architectural features, a front porch, and, yes, a white picket fence. If you like a country or laid-back, effortless vibe, you're probably going to lean toward Cottage as your core design. If you already live in a cottage or a bungalow, this is naturally your core design—duh!

VINTAGE CRAFTSMAN COTTAGE

EXTERIOR

Industrial Wall Sconces

Vintage-Style Brass Doorbell

Front Door Painted "Spearmint" by Sherwin-Williams

456
Art Deco House Numbers

All Trim Painted "Pure White" by Sherwin-Williams

Front Door Light

Maintenance-Free Decking

Matte Black Handleset with Electronic Keypad

Flowering Tree in Front Yard

Exterior House Paint Color "Grizzle Gray" by Sherwin-Williams

Cheery Front Door Inspiration

VINTAGE CRAFTSMAN COTTAGE

BASICS

Sleek Ceiling Fan

Neutral Woven Window Shades

Custom Craftsman-Style Doors

Brass Toilet-Paper Holders

Vintage-Style Doorknobs

Inspiration

Traditional Elongated Toilets

Antique Brass Cabinet Hardware

Original Floors Refinished

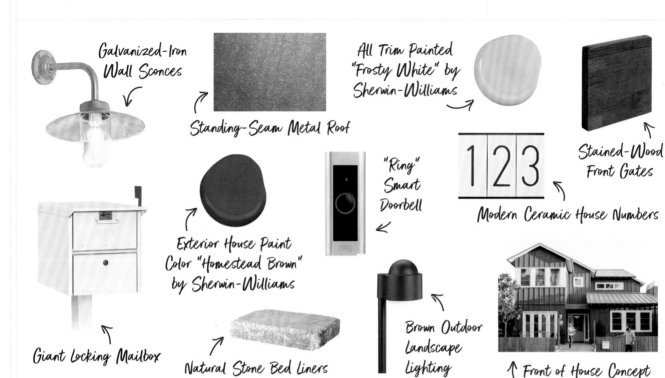

TRADITIONAL INDUSTRIAL HOMESTEAD

EXTERIOR

Galvanized-Iron Wall Sconces

Standing-Seam Metal Roof

All Trim Painted "Frosty White" by Sherwin-Williams

Stained-Wood Front Gates

"Ring" Smart Doorbell

Modern Ceramic House Numbers

Exterior House Paint Color "Homestead Brown" by Sherwin-Williams

Giant Locking Mailbox

Natural Stone Bed Liners

Brown Outdoor Landscape Lighting

Front of House Concept

TRADITIONAL INDUSTRIAL HOMESTEAD

BASICS

Sleek Fan

House Plant

Solid-Core White Doors

Simple Toilet-Paper Holders

Black Framed Windows

Matte Black Door Hardware

Interior Concept

Elongated Toilets

Brushed Brass Cabinet & Drawer Pulls

Whiskey Oak Floors Upstairs

Traditional

Calling all lovers of Cape Cod, Tudor, Colonial, and historic homes! If you live in one of those already, or maybe you really want to emulate a more refined style in your home, then Traditional is calling your name. Think of more prominent, detailed architectural elements, like millwork and built-in bookcases. To me, Traditional style nowadays feels like a modern-day Craftsman home.

Rustic

If you're all about homes that feel lived in while using a lot of natural materials and more organic tones and textures, then Rustic style is for you. If you live in a home that's Spanish or Tuscan style or maybe even a farmhouse, this is your core design. Exposed wooden beams, plaster walls, or reclaimed wooden interior siding would be found in Rustic homes, as would more timeworn materials.

RUSTIC VINTAGE CABIN EXTERIOR

Outdoor Inspiration ↑

Weathered Copper Outdoor Lighting

Front Door Painted "White Heron" by Sherwin-Williams

Post Lighting as Needed

Painted Fascia & Window Trim

Durable Patio Furniture

Rustic Railings

Cozy Firepit ↑

Low-Maintenance Plantings

Exterior Painted "Black Beauty" by Benjamin Moore

Organic Pea Gravel in → Landscaping

RUSTIC VINTAGE CABIN BASICS

Natural Materials on Accent Walls

Simple Organic Furniture

DONT GIVE UP THE SHIP

↑ Organic Art

Simple Toilet-Paper Holders

Wall Sconce Task Lighting

Handcrafted Bathroom Lighting

Kitchen Inspiration

Timeless Kitchen Accessories

Woodburning Stove ↗

Bathroom Inspiration ↑

Style Add-Ons

Now that you've narrowed down and identified your core design, let's get even more specific. Each of the core designs can have several style add-ons. These are the more focused, detail-oriented descriptions that will inform the more nitpicky aspects of your design. Understanding these style add-ons will really help you focus on how you want your home to feel—and they'll even help you shop for furnishings and accessories!

And just like when you picked your core design, I want you to keep in mind that the focus is on how these styles are thought of *today*. Many of these terms have historically rooted, technical definitions, but I'm using them in more of a designer sense. If you hire a contractor or carpenter to help with your project, these terms will ring true as modern-day adaptations, unless you specify that you want a more technical representation of the style.

With your core design selected, you now need to choose one to three style add-ons. If your core design is the jeans and classic white T-shirt of your design, then the style add-ons are what make the outfit a bit funkier. They're the jacket, the shoes, and everything that makes the look more personal. This whole combination will ensure your design feels multidimensional and just like you! Read through these style add-ons in the next few pages and see what you react to the most strongly. The answer may surprise you!

Cape Cod

When it comes to architecture, Cape Cod homes have a very specific, recognizable look. But that vibe can be applied to interior design as well. Beadboard or board-and-batten siding on the interior walls, usually painted white, really convey Cape Cod design. Furniture and accessories lean Traditional, and blue tones or stripes are commonly used on textiles in these airy, slightly beachy spaces.

Industrial

If you're into exposed ceilings or find beauty in raw materials such as iron, original brick, and visible pipes, you have Industrial design leanings. Maybe you like more open spaces instead of designated rooms? Then the kitchen and the dining space and the living area are all one large space. Maybe you like soaring ceilings where you can see all the ductwork? Industrial design celebrates those building materials and elements that you'd find in a factory or warehouse.

Craftsman

Craftsman style typically goes hand in hand with California style—it's an architecture style that originated in California in the 1890s, so it feels very West Coast in spirit. If we're talking about the outside, a Craftsman home would have a covered porch with square columns and lots of decorative braces in the roofing. On the inside, Craftsman style would have plenty of handcrafted details, built-in custom carpentry such as bookcases, and a slightly more open floor plan than, say, Cape Cod or Colonial styles. True traditional Craftsman interiors focused on natural wood and earthy tones throughout, but nowadays modern Craftsman interiors can be airier and more neutral in color.

Midcentury Modern

This is a style many of us are familiar with by now (thanks, *Mad Men*!). It was very popular from the 1940s to the 1960s, and it has been making a major comeback for the last several years. Think clean lines, earthy tones, and slightly rounded furniture edges. Brass and wood are big materials for this style. Midcentury Modern style can also feel more minimally decorated than other trends, and it's important to note that furniture in this style is usually lower to the ground.

Colonial

This is a style that takes it way back to times of grand entryways with curving staircases and spectacular floral wallpapers. If you're all about wainscoting, millwork, and trim detailing just about everywhere, you have some Colonial in your house story. Colonial homes feel like they're steeped in history, and they're perfect for someone who classifies their style as being more Traditional.

Farmhouse

If your style leans more Rustic, the super-popular farmhouse style might be right for you. Farmhouse style is known for salvaged items—think of reclaimed wooden beams, a door from an old barn, or a 100-year-old hutch with chipped paint. Current takes on Farmhouse usually have a lot of white in the design with black accents. This style should feel effortlessly lived in. The more wear and tear on something, the better. This pairs nicely with Industrial elements, too, so if that also ticks your boxes, then you're in for a winning combo!

Scandinavian

Scandinavian interiors are typically neutral in color palette and very minimally decorated. They're bright and airy spaces with lots of light-toned wood and white used in the design. This is a look that feels both sleek and warm at the same time, and that's usually achieved by using lots of organic textures. If you don't like clutter *at all*, this is the style for you!

Vintage

If you've got a more Vintage style, you're probably at the thrift store or antique market every weekend, hunting for older pieces with character. You're not too concerned with everything "matching," and when it comes to decor, the older the better. You'd rather have a 100-year-old kitchen table than a brand-new one.

Organic

If you feel one with nature and have plants sprinkled throughout your house, you're probably going to be into Organic style. Design-wise this means varying wood tones (and some live-edge wood for good measure), jute and rope elements, and a good dose of canvas. Woven wall hangings make total sense in an organic design, as do rustic pottery pieces in earthy colors. This is a style that is easy to fuse into other styles because it simply requires that you lean heavily into more natural elements. For example, my California casual design aesthetic is deeply rooted in Organic style.

Spanish

If you're all about chunky exposed-wood beams in the ceiling and large amounts of natural stone, you're probably into Spanish style. Spanish style also tends to lean on an earthy color palette and more organic textures and tones. This style feels decidedly Rustic and usually incorporates details such as wrought iron, arched doorways, and intricate colorful tiles.

Boho

When I think of Boho (or bohemian) style, I think of FUN. Boho style is full of life and personality, and to achieve this look you should go for vibrant colors, layered patterns, shaggy textures, and lots of plants. Oh, and rattan! Don't forget rattan—or any type of woven baskets, really. Boho and Organic styles go hand in hand, so feel free to put those two together, if it strikes your fancy.

Tudor

As far as Tudor style goes, in my experience, this usually is reflected in the exterior look of a home rather than in current interior design trends. If you already live in a Tudor-style home and want to have your interior match this more traditional architecture style, aim for the inside of your home to have wood detailing in the ceiling with a darker wood tone. Think of traditional English design when picking furniture pieces. A four-poster bed would be right at home in a Tudor-style space, as would a delicate light fixture.

Cabin

Cabin style is all about texture and cozy vibes. The more Rustic elements, the better. If you wished you lived in the woods or the mountains somewhere, you're probably into Cabin style. Exposed raw-wood elements, plaid or tartan fabrics, and a generally unfussy spirit are all present in Cabin-style spaces.

Tuscan

Tuscan style is focused on evoking an Italian countryside feeling, so if you prefer rough plaster walls, wood-beam ceilings, and terra-cotta floors, this look is for you. Earthy colors are the star in Tuscan spaces, and wrought-iron details are another telltale sign. Above all, homes with Tuscan style are usually very rustic and welcoming.

Be Realistic

Diving into style is super fun, but next we need to get our ducks in a row. Before we go any further, take into account what you see around you. I'm talking about your neighbor's house, if you have a homeowner's association (HOA), your neighborhood's aesthetic, if you're renting an apartment, etc. Think of the organic cues you receive from your area—are you by the beach? Are you in the woods? If you live in an apartment in the middle of San Francisco, your considerations will be different than a person who lives in a 200-year-old farmhouse in rural Pennsylvania. Do you have those cues top of mind? Okay, moving on.

Real Life versus Dream Life

For years I've met with clients who have no clue where to start. On pages 30 and 31 is a version of a consultation I do with clients that you can do with yourself—if you're really honest and think through each question, identifying your house story should be really easy. So here goes. You're my client and we're meeting on Day 1 of our renovation. Help me get to know you first so I can help design your house.

By answering these questions, you'll have a well-rounded approach to your project instead of just thinking about style. Sometimes style means more than just what you see. Approach your project from a realistic point of view. You've read about all those cool design styles and you're stoked, but you also don't want to pick a style that won't function with your daily life. But you *do* want a style that makes you happy. So, let's bridge your real life with your dream life. . . .

Real Life
WORKSHEET

The answers to these questions will point you toward your
core design.

- Where do you currently live?

- Are you in a city setting or somewhere rural?

- Are you in the mountains or on the beach? In the suburbs?

- Who do you live with?

- Do you rent or own?

- Do you have an HOA?

- What type of home do you live in? Single-family residence,
  apartment, townhome, or mobile home?

- How old is your home?

- How would you describe your home's exterior style?

- How would you describe your home's interior style?

- What's one thing in your home you wouldn't change?

- What's one thing in your home you would absolutely change?

Dream Life
WORKSHEET

The answers to these questions will point you toward your style add-ons.

- Where do you wish you lived?

- Is there somewhere you've traveled that you wish you could stay for the rest of your life? What drew you to the place?

- Do you prefer sparse, minimal, clean spaces?

- What would you be happy to see when you walk through the door from work or wherever?

- How would you use your home on a dream weekend?

- Do you want to entertain?

- Do you like spaces that feel new, spaces that feel old, or something in between?

- Where would you shop for your house if you didn't have to think about anyone else or a budget?

- What's a style you could live with long-term?

The Formula

The goal of this book is to help you bridge your dream life and your real life so you have a home that makes you happy and gives you the function that you need. I call this your house story! To nail down your house story, pick your core design and one to three style add-ons. Your answers from the Real Life Worksheet (page 30) will help you confirm what your home's existing core design is. The Real Life Worksheet will also guide you in figuring out how your home needs to function for everyone who lives there.

Your Dream Life Worksheet (page 31) will point you to the specific style add-ons that will lift up your core design and infuse your home with personality. The Dream Life Worksheet answers will shine a light on those design details that give you butterflies and put a smile on your face.

Once you identify your house story, use it throughout your whole home so that your space feels cohesive. Try to stick to this style for every room (don't go rogue!); otherwise it gets a bit tricky, and I'm all about keeping it simple. So, go ahead and take your real life and mix it with your dream life—that hybrid is your personal house story. You're welcome!

CLIENT 1: Contemporary, Organic, Midcentury Modern

This home feels like California's interpretation of an easy, breezy Midcentury Modern design. The classic MidMod cues are all there, with clean lines and features such as sleek tile floors and an open-concept floor plan, with organic textures and the spirit of laid-back coastal living added in. This is a home to two little kids and two dogs, so the open floor plan and clean lines also are true to how this family needs their home to function.

CLIENT 2: Craftsman Cottage with Vintage Accents

This sweet little home has telltale Craftsman nods from the exterior while marrying bungalow and Vintage details throughout the interior. A classic white kitchen with a farmhouse sink, sliding barn door in the master bath, and handmade vintage pieces round out this nostalgic home.

CLIENT 3: Rustic Organic Cabin

Located on a lake, this Vintage cabin was all wood paneling and zero style. The homeowners decided to embrace the handcrafted details and pair them with modern appliances, while keeping the feel of a summer camp. The end result is a Rustic space that has character and celebrates nature.

Now it's your turn!

One core design
+ one to three style add-ons
= your house story.

My house story: _____

Use this as your compass as you go through the rest of this book. If you stick to your house story and always default to things that fall within it, at the end of your project, you'll find yourself in a cohesive space that just feels right.

Jazzy's CHAPTER 1 CHECKLIST

☐ Did you define your house story?

☐ Were you honest and realistic about your current living situation?

☐ Are you ready to stick to your style to make your house awesome?

If you answered "no" to any of the above, you have more work to do! Flip back to page 12, read through the core designs and style add-ons again, and redo your Real Life Worksheet. Be brutally honest this time and commit to your outcome. I promise different things will jump out to you when you read through the styles again.

2

CURB APPEAL—IT'S WHAT'S ON THE OUTSIDE THAT COUNTS

"The decisions we make about our home's design and functionality form the foundation of our house story."

It's time to address an all-too-often neglected part of home renovation and transformation: curb appeal. If you own your home, the land your home sits on is half of what is likely the biggest investment of your life, and for many, it's an afterthought. Curb appeal is the first way anyone experiences your house, and it sets the tone for how you feel when you come home. In this chapter, we'll break it down slowly (like a super-slow-motion version of my show) and explain what's going on behind that 30-second just-back-from-the-commercial-break reveal you see on television.

Front Doors

The front door says something about who lives there, so what's your door going to say? It's a great design opportunity to set the tone of your house story.

Understanding the Front Door

Solid Plank

Paneled

Dutch

Arched

Half Glass

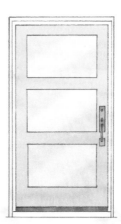

Full Glass

Functionality

What type of front door is right for your home? Well, before you go and pick one at random, you need to answer some questions—I know, more questions! But these are important. When you answered the Real Life Worksheet questions, you had to think about your area's organic cues, and choosing a front door is no different. If you live in an area that gets a lot of snow and harsh weather, you probably shouldn't go with a Dutch door—I hate to break it to you. Yes, they're super adorable, but they aren't practical for places that get the full force of Mother Nature from time to time. So, if you live in an area with a more temperate climate, go for the Dutch door. A glass door, whether it's full glass or half glass, would work well in homes that don't need a lot of privacy. You get the idea.

But don't get discouraged! Even with some restrictions as to which doors will work on your house, you can still have fun with the front door. Arched doors are beautiful and add a lot of whimsy to the front of your home, and you can ensure they're thick enough to insulate your home on the coldest of days. Solid plank and paneled doors can also be really lovely and draw interest to your curb appeal, whether you use a gorgeous wood or paint the door in an eye-catching color. If you live someplace where it's really cold in the winter and really hot in the summer, you can still experience some of those Dutch door vibes by using a practical door (like paneled or solid plank) and installing a screen.

Hardware Types and Tech Upgrades

Before you fall asleep, I promise that this door hardware stuff is actually kinda fun! Your front door isn't going to look right if you go through all the trouble of establishing your house story everywhere but your door. Take the time to pay attention to these details, and you won't regret it.

This seems like a no-brainer, but you need to measure your door before ordering hardware. You'd be surprised to know how many times this step is skipped! Not all doors and hardware are created equal, so measuring is key here. Exterior doors can come in different thicknesses, so you'll want to make sure your chosen hardware works with your door. Then select your hardware—the result will be a mix of personal preference and following your style. Some people prefer a knob, others like a lever handle. Identify what finish would work best and then source hardware options in that finish. For instance, matte black hardware would look nice on a more modern home or even an updated cottage with industrial or contemporary accents. Once you've identified that matte black is the finish you need, you can narrow down the hardware type based on preference. There are so many kinds of hardware available these days that the difference between knob or lever won't dictate your style as much as the finish will. So, focus on the finish to really drive home your style and then select what will feel the most satisfying to you when you open and close your front door every day.

Jazzy's FAVORITE HARDWARE RESOURCES

Baldwin

Build.com

Emtek

Hardware stores such as Home Depot or Lowe's

Rejuvenation

Pro tip: Purchase your door hardware in a set, meaning that the handle, hinges, peephole, and lock set all come from the same manufacturer. If you hire a contractor for your job, make sure you're on the same page with the hardware set before they make any purchases. You may not have thought of this, but the hinges need to match the hardware set. Trust me: it looks silly if they don't match. So, have the conversation with your contractor early on to communicate your finish (that is, matte black, oil-rubbed bronze, or brass and so on) so they don't hang your door with whatever they have lying around. I've seen it happen many times! Cobbling together pieces that appear the same but aren't from the same manufacturer usually looks off.

If you want to take security and function to the next level, an electronic keypad is a total game-changer. You don't have to carry a key, and you can set different codes for different people. I like the brand Schlage, and the one you get from your local hardware store is perfect—you don't have to spend a fortune.

Colors and Finishes

Front door colors can make or break a house. Since your front door's paint color is something you can easily change, it's worth trying what you like—even if you don't get it right at the first crack. Color is a great way to both evoke feeling and carry through your style. Choosing the right color for your home can be easy if you follow your already determined core design and pay attention to your exterior paint color and the organic cues around your home.

Pro Tip: I paint only the outside of the door a color and leave ALL TRIM and the inside white. This makes the front door really pop!

Jazzy's
FAVORITE FRONT-DOOR COLORS

When it comes to picking the right paint color for your front door, I truly believe that whatever color you choose will look great because it's your home and it's all about what *you* like. But in case you take a look at this list of colors and get overwhelmed, I've got you covered. I made a shortcut with tried-and-true color pairings for each of the core designs, so you can just plug and play.

CONTEMPORARY

BENJAMIN MOORE:
HC-154 HALE NAVY

BENJAMIN MOORE:
2028-30 TEQUILA LIME

SHERWIN-WILLIAMS:
SW 6211 RAINWASHED

SHERWIN-WILLIAMS:
SW 7642 PAVESTONE

SHERWIN-WILLIAMS:
SW 9059 SILKEN PEACOCK

COTTAGE

SHERWIN-WILLIAMS:
SW 6941 NIFTY TURQUOISE

SHERWIN-WILLIAMS:
SW 9050 VINTAGE VESSEL

SHERWIN-WILLIAMS:
SW 6837 BARONESS

SHERWIN-WILLIAMS:
SW 7600 BOLERO

SHERWIN-WILLIAMS:
SW 7641 COLONNADE GRAY

TRADITIONAL

SHERWIN-WILLIAMS:
SW 6258 TRICORN BLACK

SHERWIN-WILLIAMS:
SW 7641 COLONNADE GRAY

DUNN EDWARDS:
DE 5390 RUBBER DUCKY

SHERWIN-WILLIAMS:
SW 6509 GEORGIAN BAY

SHERWIN-WILLIAMS:
SW 0044 HUBBARD SQUASH

RUSTIC

SHERWIN-WILLIAMS:
SW 6356 COPPER MOUNTAIN

SHERWIN-WILLIAMS:
SW 9059 SILKEN PEACOCK

SHERWIN-WILLIAMS:
SW 6465 SPEARMINT

SHERWIN-WILLIAMS:
SW 9168 ELEPHANT EAR

SHERWIN-WILLIAMS:
SW 7061 NIGHT OWL

The Special Details

There's a way to really unlock the hidden potential (see what I did there?!) of your curb appeal, and it's through personalization. If you devote the same attention to your front exterior as you do the inside of your house, your curb appeal will shine. I'm talking about front door decals, welcome mats, mailboxes, house numbers, potted plants, vintage embellishments, and more. All of these details can enhance your house story and let your personality shine through to anyone passing by.

Maybe you choose a mailbox that's totally unconventional or house numbers that are mounted on a succulent planter, or maybe you have your favorite flowers potted on either side of your walkway that leads up to a "I hope you brought wine" doormat. All of these details are opportunities to infuse your personality and make your home feel special.

OUTDOOR LIGHTING

Light it up! Lighting is one of those things that you don't really think about until it's dark out—but it's so important for curb appeal. You and your guests should be able to walk up to your home at nighttime as easily as you do during the day. Two things achieve that: ample front porch lighting and strategically placed walkway or sidewalk lighting. Place path lights in the planters on the side of your sidewalk or pavers every 4 to 6 feet. For the front door area, make sure you install a bright enough light overhead so you can safely find your keys. If it's not an option to install porch lighting overhead at the front of your home, consider installing a post light near the door so you can see clearly when someone's at your door. Adding up-lighting to trees in the front yard will also do wonders for making the front of your home feel warm and inviting at night.

Landscaping

Can you remember the last time you saw a home with lackluster landscaping? No, you probably can't, because bad landscaping is never memorable! It's kind of the opposite of that saying about wedding DJs—"you only remember the bad DJs"—because if a DJ is playing hit after hit all night, all you remember is being on the dance floor and having fun! So, let's just swap the DJs and landscaping thing here and make landscaping *fun*. Truly, though, when landscaping isn't considered, it really hurts a home's curb appeal. And there's nothing fun about that.

I think a lot of homeowners feel intimidated when it comes to landscaping, because they think you need to be some sort of plant wizard to pull off a cohesive look. If you've ever been to a nursery, you've probably felt how overwhelming it is to see the dizzying world of plant and flower possibilities. But I've actually invented a trick that is super easy to pull off, and it's worked on every project I've ever done.

Enter my Rule of Three: Pick one accent color and two shades of green—and stick to it! Use those same three tones and plants throughout the whole project, and it will feel cohesive and look great. So, for example, if your Rule of Three includes a light shade of green, a dark shade of green, and purple as your accent color, don't show up to the nursery and grab lavender *and* red begonias *and* yellow forsythia plants. But *do* choose purple flowers or flowering shrubs of different kinds, because they will all flow together.

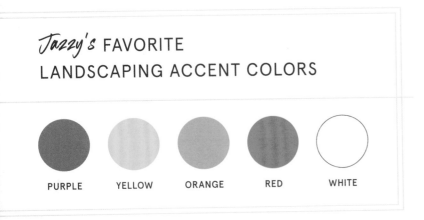

Jazzy's FAVORITE
LANDSCAPING ACCENT COLORS

PURPLE   YELLOW   ORANGE   RED   WHITE

Make It a Room—Outdoor Living!

The key to outdoor awesomeness and really, truly getting the most use out of your outdoor area is to treat it like a room! That's right—whether you have a patio, a porch, a backyard, or a little patch of grass off to the side of your home, designing your outdoor area as if it were an actual room in your house will make all the difference in the world. Reminder: Before you even get started, make sure you have your house story in mind and stick to it.

First, start with a base. Pea gravel, an outdoor rug, stenciled concrete—whatever it may be, ensure you create a base area to anchor your outdoor chill zone. Then it's time to add in some really comfy seating. If it's not comfortable, you won't want to be out there as much. So, go for the outdoor couch, oversize chairs, and a cool outdoor coffee table where you can put up your feet or set down a drink. Set the mood with shade options and pretty lighting. You don't want to be roasting in the sun, and you also don't want to be sitting in the dark. Look for umbrellas that match your style, or you might even consider adding a pergola if it's in your budget. String up some bulb lights, find a cute outdoor lamp, or invest in some lanterns to create a beautiful and relaxing nighttime vibe. Then, since we're encouraging maximum fun and entertainment, add something that takes the space to the next level and engages your family and guests. Think of an oversize Jenga set, a porch swing, or some sort of lawn game.

For all your decisions in designing this outdoor room, make sure you choose decor that's an extension of your indoor decor and style. Aim for different patterns and textures to amplify the comfort of your outdoor space, while keeping the color palette similar to the inside of your home. By doing this, your outdoor space will feel like a seamless connection to the rest of the home and welcome you outside time and time again.

What Now? Okay, I've given you lots of advice and options, but how do you choose? You already know what I'm going to say—stick to your house story! Use your curb appeal to introduce your style and set the tone for the rest of the house. For example, if your style is Contemporary Organic Midcentury Modern, you might already have a more modern house to begin with. Using a reclaimed wooden front door with a black hammered-metal pull would be a great way to accomplish that Organic part of your design and set the tone for the rest of the project. Or maybe you have a cottage that feels drab and boring—but you're not drab and boring! Painting your front door and adding lush landscaping can make all the difference and set the color palette for the rest of the project. And if you live in a neighborhood with an HOA or in an apartment building, and it's killing you that you can't touch your front door, don't worry! There are so many other ways to add curb appeal so your home's exterior feels special and unique every day. Just make sure it all fits within your style (think Modern versus Traditional planters, Contemporary versus script house numbers, or a Vintage versus a Modern mailbox), and you'll be good to go!

Take your core designs and style add-ons and make your curb appeal your own! Layer in your personal touches through easy-to-change accents and decor. For example, a seasonal doormat, a brightly colored pot with a plant that reminds you of your last vacation, or a vintage doorbell that was on your grandma's house and makes you smile. It's okay to mix and match as long as it makes you happy!

Jazzy's CHAPTER 2 CHECKLIST

☐ Did you stick with your house story while upping the curb appeal of your house?

☐ Were you honest and realistic about your current living situation? (Don't forget about bugs and snow!)

☐ Are you ready to stick to this style to make your house awesome?

If you answered "no" to any of the above, you have more work to do!

3

KNOCKING DOWN WALLS—THE LAYOUT LOWDOWN

"Sometimes changing a home's layout or floor plan is the game-changer you always needed to truly love your home."

Whether you're kicking off major construction or moving your bed to the opposite wall of your room to maximize floor space, this chapter is all about rethinking. Take everything you know and throw it out the window! You know how on TV we have those animated graphics in which the walls melt into the floor and kitchen islands seem to sprout from below? Well, this is where I teach you how to see that for your own space. Cool, right?

Now, before you start swinging that sledgehammer and daydreaming of disappearing walls, I have some homework for you! It's time to answer some realistic questions about how you live and how you plan to use your space (see The Floor Plan Worksheet on page 68). It might seem like you've thought about these things, but trust me, this is a tremendous help and a necessary step to designing your dream home.

the FLOOR PLAN WORKSHEET

THE PEOPLE

- Who currently lives in your home?

- Who will live in your home in five years? In ten years?

- Do you have pets in your home?

- Does anyone play an instrument in your home? Will anyone?

- Who takes baths in your home? Who will?

- Does anyone in your house work from home?

- Do you homeschool?

THE STUFF

- What's your favorite thing to do inside?

- What's your favorite thing to do outside?

- What's a room you can't live without?

- What's a room you could get rid of?

- Do you need air-conditioning?

- Do you cook often?

- Do you have a grand piano?

- Are you able to buy a new couch or other large furniture, or do you need to work with what you have?

THE TIME

- When do you spend time at your home?

- When do others spend time at your home?

- When do you feel most relaxed?

- When do you feel most anxious about your home?

THE LOCATION

- Do you need wheelchair access?

- Do you need a security system?

- Do you need a fence?

- Do you need privacy?

- Do you want space to entertain?

- Do you live near water?

- Do you live where snow is common?

THE BIG PICTURE

- What must be changed today?

- What can wait to be changed?

- What do you never want to change?

- What can increase resale value for the future?

The Cold, Hard Truth about Knocking Down Walls

On my TV shows, you see me say, "Let's take down a wall!" And 30 seconds later, the wall is down. Like magic! But in real life, it doesn't work like that. It's important to understand just how much work knocking down a wall can be. Whether it's digging a hole to underpin a footing to increase its size or adding new beams in the ceiling and reframing pretty much everything, it's going to be a huge project. If any part of that last sentence made you say, "huh?" that means you definitely shouldn't try to do this yourself. Removing a wall from your home is always a big undertaking, and as a project it's almost never all buttoned up the next day, let alone the same week. It's a REALLY BIG DEAL, folks. It's also not always possible to remove a wall from your home. Walls are often built into homes for a reason (*shocking, I know!*), and some of them are just straight up not negotiable. Some walls hold up most of the house or contain plumbing and electrical, and you just can't touch them. So, before you go around your house with your ear pressed to each wall, knocking on them to see if they're load-bearing, listen up: that's not a thing. No, really! Knocking on a wall won't tell you if it's load-bearing or not. So, before you get any pie-in-the-sky ideas about knocking a wall down and opening up your floor plan, just wait until you meet with an engineer and a general contractor.

If you're sitting there at home crossing "knock down wall" off your now tear-stained remodel wish list, chin up! I'm not telling you all this to scare and discourage you—I just want you to be as informed and prepared as possible so you can have a successful remodel and realistic expectations. DON'T DISTRESS!

Chatting with a Contractor? Here's What You Should Ask.

Now that you know the truth about knocking down walls, let's talk about the timeline. When you meet with your contractor to discuss changing your layout, ask them, "What can I realistically expect to be living with, and how long until everything is finished?" Ask them what the process will entail so you can wrap your head around the entire project. And take it from me, you're probably going to want to move out for a little while.

Most of the time when a wall is removed, you'll need to add new flooring, new drywall, new lighting, new electrical, and so on to accommodate the loss of the wall. Basically, your house will be completely torn apart. I told you, it's a big deal. And nine times out of ten, an engineer will need to redo the framing calculations before you even get started. Hiring an engineer will be an added cost and can also impact your timeline based on their availability to come to your work site. So, make sure you ask your contractor if you need to hire an engineer for your project and, if so, pad your budget ahead of time to accommodate for the potential cost.

And last but not least, before you get started, ask your contractor what could possibly be discovered when they take down the wall—and how much it would cost to address those incidentals. You know on the show when we rip the drywall off the wall and I yell, "Oh, $*@&" when I see what's inside? And then we usually cut to commercials and when we come back, it's all figured out—TV MAGIC! Well, in real life, it doesn't work like that. There are days (if not weeks), not to mention added costs, spent trying to deal with what you find. So, yeah, surprises are great sometimes, but in the world of construction and home renovation, the fewer surprises, the better.

The Layout Lowdown

Layout got you down? Let's fix that! Sometimes changing a home's layout or floor plan is the game-changer you always needed to truly love your home. Maybe you've outgrown your home's layout since you moved in. Or maybe you're taking over a new-to-you home with a layout that doesn't quite work. Either way, maximizing how your home functions for you is essential. Most of my clients needed to reimagine their home, but they were stuck. After living in your home, it's hard to picture it any other way! And for each project, I showed them how to see the potential within their home to change for the better. In many of those homes, what we needed was to knock down a wall that was cutting off the flow of the house or

move a wall back to expand a kitchen or add a walk-in closet. In some houses I've actually *added* walls. That's right! People grow and change over time, and so do your needs for your home. Maybe your open-concept space worked great when you needed to see your little ones, but now that they're teenagers it might make sense to add some walls to give them their own dedicated hangout spot.

I know what you're thinking—this sounds great, but how in the world do I get started? Let's break down five common needs for a layout makeover, and I'll change the floor plan to accommodate each scenario. I'm giving you the super-slow-motion, behind-the-scenes look of my home remodeling show, but this isn't on TV! No need to hit pause—I'm showing you side-by-side floor plans of the "before" and "after" so you can get the ideas you need to reimagine your own home!

Five Different Layout Scenarios

Whether you're adding a wall or taking one down, sometimes it just takes a little vision to see how your space can function better for you. Each one of these clients was stumped, but the answer was right in front of them. Check out these examples to see if one of them can solve a layout problem for you!

EXAMPLE 1: Opening up a kitchen and adding an island.

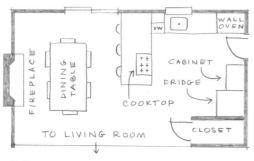

Before

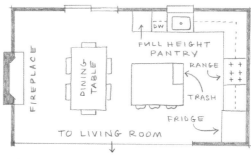

After

EXAMPLE 2: Adding a walk-in closet and desk area to a primary bedroom.

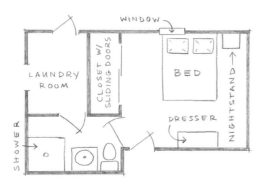

Before

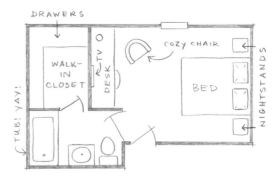

After

EXAMPLE 3: Opening up a big, compartmentalized home; making the kitchen "eat-in" while also adding double islands and a dining banquette.

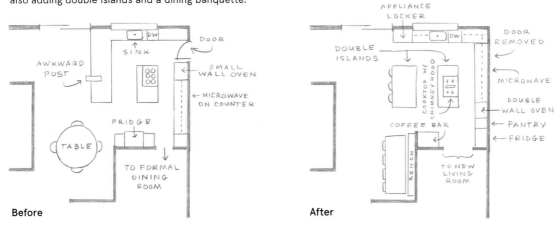

Before

After

EXAMPLE 4: Adding walls to a more open home to accommodate growing teenagers who need their own space, a work-from-home office, and a guest bedroom.

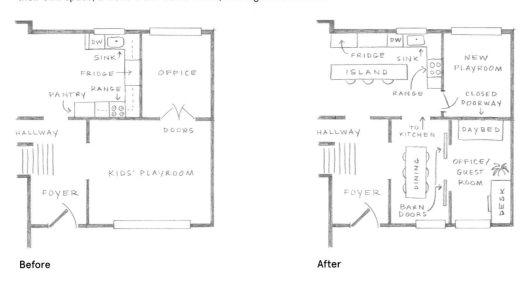

Before

After

EXAMPLE 5: Changing sight lines in the home to see young kids from other spaces and see from the front of the home all the way through to the back.

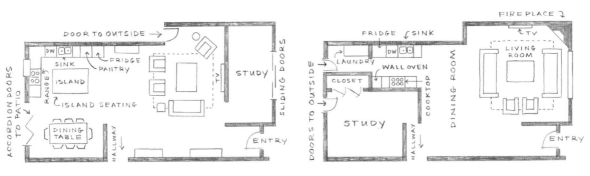

Before

After

The Same Space, Three Ways, *Furniture Only*

If you can't move or take down any walls, no problem. There's so much that can be maximized in a space by simply moving the furniture around. Yes, even furniture layout can be functional. And functionality is key, people! Even just one really functional piece of furniture can change everything.

PRIMARY BEDROOM

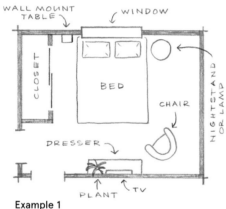

Example 1

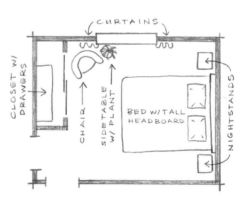

Example 2

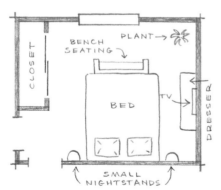

Example 3

LIVING ROOM

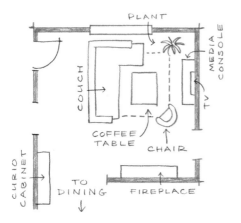

Example 1

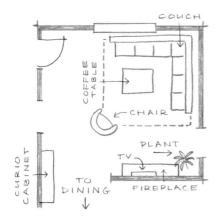

Example 2

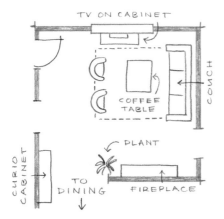

Example 3

SECONDARY BEDROOM

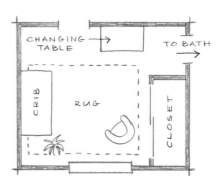

Example 1: Nursery

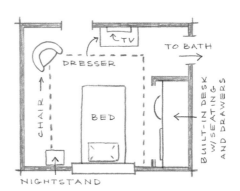

Example 2: Guest room

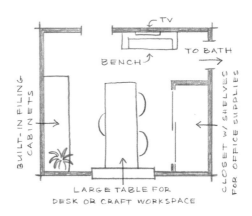

Example 3: Home Office

Jazzy's CHAPTER 3 CHECKLIST

☐ Did the worksheet make you think of something you hadn't considered before?

☐ Did you check in with your contractor or engineer; or if you're moving furniture, how do the other people in your house feel about it?

☐ Is there an opportunity to use a piece of furniture to make an EPIC change that you just haven't thought of yet? (This is a trick question— there's ALWAYS a piece of furniture that can make things better!)

If you answered "no" to any of the above, you have more work to do!

4

WALL TREATMENTS AND FLOOR FINISHES— THE FOUNDATION OF YOUR HOUSE STORY

"I want your home to be livable, functional, beautiful, and incredibly personal. I want you to be comfortable in your home."

When it comes to major decisions such as floors and walls, "keep it simple" is my motto. These are big-ticket items so I'm partial to white ceilings, a single neutral wall color (like Dunn Edwards "Faded Gray"), and timeless (not trendy) floors. Floors and walls are the BASE of any good design, and they're important! But when I say to keep it simple, I actually mean spend a lot of time figuring this out, be intentional, and never underestimate the power of a great wall treatment or awesome accent floor. Where to start? Let's talk walls first, then we'll chat floors.

The Basics— Choosing Wall Colors

Your walls and ceilings are drywall 99 percent of the time. That means they need to be painted, and one of the first things you'll need to decide is a paint color. Have you ever walked into the hardware store in a great mood, thinking you're going to find the perfect paint color and paint your walls that same day, only to leave discouraged and overwhelmed, with twenty-five little pieces of colored paper (these are called paint chips) and some paint supplies that you don't even know how to use? I have! So, I'm sharing some advice on how to choose paint colors and then paint your walls. Oh, and just because I know you're going to ask, I use the same wall color throughout the entire house. The bedroom, kitchen, and bathroom walls are all the same color. Don't pick a different color for each room (unless you really have a vision), because your house could end up feeling like one of those fun houses at the carnival. However, if you want to mix it up a bit, try an accent wall! That's when you paint one wall a different color. More on that on page 88.

Testing Paint

You can very rarely choose paint colors on the first try. It's just a fact—paint looks different in each space, and yours is no exception. What looks awesome online might look terrible in your house. For example, I may love a light gray color that I see on an online blog (Jenny Komenda gives *great* paint recommendations on her blog, *Juniper Home*—hey, Jenny!), but when I try that same paint on my walls, it might come across as super pink, or tan, or even worse—gasp!—purple. It's important to get a few different options, paint them on big pieces of craft board or right onto the walls, let them dry, and then see how they look. You also need to let the sun do its thing—paint colors look different throughout the day and with different weather. So, yeah, this isn't a one-hour process that you can finish up in one trip to the hardware store. Sorry!

Jazzy's
FAVORITE INTERIOR PAINT COLORS

DUNN EDWARDS:
DEW 382 FADED GRAY

SHERWIN-WILLIAMS:
SW 7004 SNOWBOUND

SHERWIN-WILLIAMS:
SW 7015 REPOSE GRAY

SHERWIN-WILLIAMS:
SW 7631 CITY LOFT

SHERWIN-WILLIAMS:
SW 7008 ALABASTER

SHERWIN-WILLIAMS:
SW 7506 LOGGIA

SHERWIN-WILLIAMS:
SW 7029 AGREEABLE GRAY

SHERWIN-WILLIAMS:
SW 7065 ARGOS

SHERWIN-WILLIAMS:
SW 7641 COLONNADE GRAY

SHERWIN-WILLIAMS:
SW 7005 PURE WHITE

My Favorite Paint Colors

Finding the perfect paint color is gratifying and will make your space feel lovely. I'll also tell you this—almost all of the houses you see on my social feeds and blog have the same wall color (Dunn Edwards "Faded Gray"), and it has worked for me 100 percent of the time. So that's somewhere to start. Opposite and below are some of my other faves.

Jazzy's FAVORITE ACCENT WALL COLORS

BENJAMIN MOORE:
2123-20 CARIBBEAN TEAL

SHERWIN-WILLIAMS:
SW 6393 CONVIVIAL YELLOW

SHERWIN-WILLIAMS:
SW 6991 BLACK MAGIC

Other Wall Options

You've identified the walls you want to paint, but you can take this project to the next level. First up, pick a wall that can add something special to the room. Usually this is called an accent wall, but I hesitate to use that description because most people think back to the '80s, when designers encouraged everyone to paint one wall in every room a different color. That's not what I'm talking about! I'm saying there might be a spot in your room where a great wall treatment would MAKE the room. But don't force it. Best way to know: There's a big blank wall staring at you, saying, "Do something cool with me!"

Once you choose your wall, think about your house story (remember that from chapter 1?) and then consider what else is going on in that room. If you have wood floors and a wood ceiling, unless you're going for a summer camp vibe, you probably don't need wood on your wall as well. Get what I'm saying? This is an opportunity to add something different to the room, a new texture, color, or even something that makes you think—so don't put on more of what's already there. That said, there aren't any rules, so have fun with your walls!

DON'T FORGET THE TRIM

In the world of baseboards, window casings, and door moldings, there are two types of trim: paint grade and stain grade. Paint grade trim gets painted. And, surprise, surprise, stain grade trim gets stained. How can you tell which one you have? Paint grade trim is usually preprimed, so it will look white. Stain grade trim usually has a raw wood finish. Most of the time, you'll find that you have paint grade trim. If you have stain grade, pick a stain color and use it throughout your entire house. Don't forget to complement your wood floors. To do so, you want to pick a stain color that's in the same tone family of your wood floors but doesn't match them exactly. Choose a stain color for your trim that's a few shades lighter or darker than the stain color of your floors. If they matched perfectly, they'd blur together when you look at them and the room wouldn't have the proper depth that comes from a bit of contrast. If you have paint grade trim, it's a little bit different.

I've got a tried-and-true formula that I stick to in almost all of my projects because it just works. The baseboards are white, the door casings are white, the window casings are white, the ceilings are the same color of white, and it looks great. Don't overthink this.

Jazzy's FAVORITE
INTERIOR TRIM
PAINT COLOR

SHERWIN-WILLIAMS:
SW 7005 PURE WHITE

Ceilings

I'm a white-ceiling, different-wall-color kinda gal. As a rule, the ceiling is usually less of an opportunity to personalize than a well-chosen accent wall, but don't ignore it! Sometimes that little extra something on the ceiling is just what a room needs. Don't forget your house story from chapter 1—your trusty friend throughout this whole project.

Okay, back to ceilings. Drawing inspiration from other places is a great jumping-off point for choosing a special ceiling treatment, but make sure it's in line with your reality. Maybe you go on vacation and see a beautiful Balinese wood ceiling in your beachside bungalow—that does NOT mean you should go home and add a teak wood ceiling to your Victorian country retreat, because that doesn't WORK! The takeaway from your great beach vacation (not just the tan) is that you might like to do *something* to a ceiling in your house—but it has to fit within your design.

Ceiling Treatments

Tongue-and-groove bleached pine kept this client's Midcentury vibe alive.

Whitewashed paneling ties in the walls of this mountain cabin.

Don't forget the sky! That's right, adding natural light can make a huge difference to your ceiling.

PAINT SHEENS

Before you head to the store and pick up any random can of paint, you need to figure out what paint sheen will work best in your space. Have you ever walked into a room and thought, "Whoa, why are these walls so . . . shiny?" That's the paint sheen talkin', folks. Please don't overlook this little detail! It makes all the difference in how beautiful your paint color can look in your space.

Satin/eggshell: This sheen is good for bathrooms or anywhere that the walls have any sort of moisture. If you have kids or high-traffic areas, you can paint your whole house in satin/eggshell. I also use this sheen on trim, doors, and moldings.

Flat: This is my go-to wall finish. I don't like shiny walls and I don't like shiny houses—do you? Probably not. Flat is the gold standard when it comes to walls and exteriors, in my humble opinion!

Semigloss: I use semigloss only on furniture—nowhere else.

Lacquer: Use lacquer on cabinets, doors, baseboards, moldings, and anything you want to be indestructible.

Still not sure which sheen is right for your paint selection? You can ask your local paint store for paint chips or samples of each sheen to see the difference.

The Basics: Choosing Flooring

Let's talk floors. As a designer, I've been asked EVERY question about flooring there is, and I'm constantly trying to keep up with new materials, installation techniques, and ideas. So, if the thought of picking your own floors overwhelms you, that's okay! This might come as a surprise, but the most important thing about picking the right floors isn't the color, the style, or even the direction that you lay them out in your house. Nope, the most important thing is picking floors that function for you and your family. That's right!

In order to figure out what floors would work best in your house, you need to think about the way you live—and be honest with yourself. Maybe you're a single gal and think you don't have to worry about which flooring you pick since the "kids/pool/dog" life isn't for you—think again! Those stiletto heels that you and your friends wear before going out at night would wreak havoc on pine hardwood floors, and you'd have to replace them quickly. Do you love to entertain and host wine nights on the regular? A porous floor material, like brick, would soak spilled wine right up and be impossible to clean! Are you a family of five with kids who love running their toy baby strollers and trucks all over the living room floor? I'd avoid expensive handmade tile or hardwood or plan to have a large rug! So, yes, there's a floor for everyone, and the first step is figuring out which floor is right for your lifestyle. And if you're out and about, pay attention to the floors in each place you visit. You never know when inspiration will strike—and when the answer will literally be right under your feet.

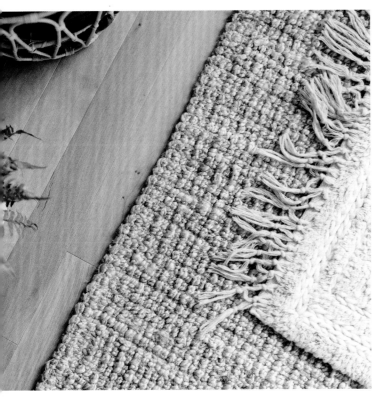

The FLOORING WORKSHEET

- Do you live by a beach or where there's a lot of snow? A carpeted entry is probably not a good idea.

- Do you run cold? Tile is probably not for you, unless it's heated.

- Would it make sense to install heated floors anywhere?

- Do you wear shoes in the house? Certain hardwoods or other materials that scratch easily may not be your best bet. Same goes for anything porous.

- Do you have kids and pets? You need something durable? Forget certain hardwood floors—they will scratch!

- Do you have stairs? Porcelain wood-look tile often doesn't have matching stair pieces. Are you willing to have a different material on your stairs than your floors?

- Do you need wet-rated floors for your kitchen, entry, and bathrooms?

- Is the flooring you've chosen for your kitchen, entry, and bathrooms slippery when wet?

- Do you have an open concept space? Is the flooring you've chosen good for all rooms within that footprint?

- How large of an area are you covering? Maybe ridiculously expensive handmade tile isn't for you.

PROS AND CONS OF FLOORING TYPES

In the wide world of flooring, there are going to be pros and cons to all types of materials. The trick is finding a material with more pros that work for your lifestyle and cons that aren't deal breakers—and hopefully you'll land on a material you'll love to have in your home. So, let's weigh the pros and cons of wood, brick, stone, tile, luxury vinyl plank flooring (known as LVP in the biz), and carpet to help you figure out what will work best for you. And since I know you're wondering, the material I use in most of my TV projects is . . . drumroll, please! . . . LVP!

WOOD

Pros

Organic texture

Ability to sand and stain a different color

Timeless

Can be durable

Cons

Can scratch

Needs special care for cleaning and maintenance

Material and installation can be expensive

BRICK

Pros

Can provide an unexpected texture

Can give an indoor/outdoor feel

Timeless

Durable

Hides dirt

Cons

Can be hard to keep clean

Porous, so it could show stains (olive oil, red wine, coffee)

Material and installation can be expensive

Can be taste specific, so not great for resale

STONE

Pros

Can be cooling

Provides an organic texture

Lasts forever, very durable

Cons

Can be cold in cooler months

Material and installation are expensive

Can be porous and could show stains (olive oil, red wine, coffee)

TILE

Pros

Not porous

Can be cooling

Durable

Many different looks can be achieved

Cons

Installation is expensive

Material is cold and hard

Grout lines can be annoying for maintenance and cleaning

LVP

Pros

Durable

Can be affordable

Looks like hardwood

Many different looks can be achieved

Installation is easy

Cons

Some brands can be slippery, so test your material

Some LVP can scratch

Prepping your floor may take more time to ensure it's even

CARPET

Pros

Soft underfoot

Keeps rooms warm in colder months

Reduces noise

Installation is easy

Safer—no slipping, and soft for children to fall on

Can be affordable

Cons

Requires lots of maintenance

Can stain or tear

Susceptible to allergens and mold, so not ideal for people with allergies

Not great for resale value

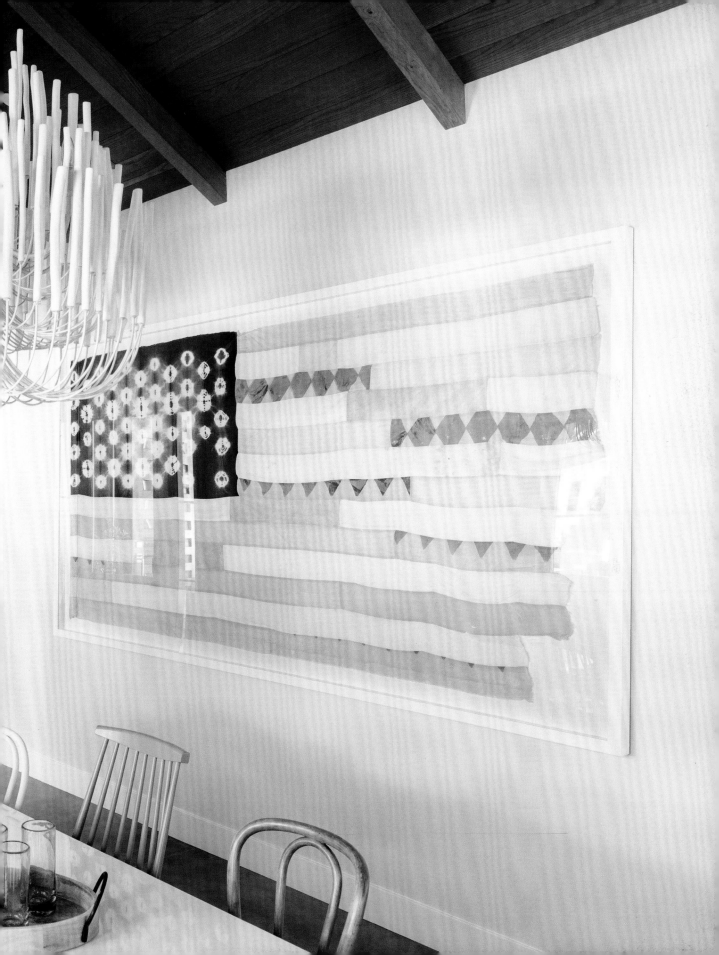

FUN FLOORS!

These might be a few fun options you can consider. Search on Google or Pinterest using these terms to get the ideas flowing.

Chevron floors	Painted floors
Herringbone floors	Polished concrete floors
Narrow plank floors	Wide plank floors

Pro tip: Order an extra box, or maybe even two, of whatever material you're installing because you never know when you're going to need some more pieces. Because flooring trends, materials, and the companies manufacturing them are constantly changing, the odds of that flooring still being manufactured a few years down the road, especially in the same colorway, are next to none.

Don't Forget the Stairs

You know those things you walk on to take you from one floor to the next? Don't overlook the stairs! They could be a great design opportunity. Stairs are a key factor in your design for two reasons: they're a canvas on which you can showcase your house story, and they need to tie in with your floors. News flash: Not all flooring types come in matching stair pieces. So, if you want your stairs to be the same material as your flooring, make sure the manufacturer makes stair pieces that match. If not, there are some really cool ways to take your stairs from a simple and timeless base to something that's personalized and unique to your style.

Before you slap some basic, boring carpet down on your stairs, take time to imagine how they could be used as a design moment. Maybe you use a pretty rug runner on your stairs instead of carpet, or maybe you stencil painted patterns onto the risers to add a beautiful and unique effect. One of my favorite options to design stairs in an unexpected way is to apply peel-and-stick wallpaper to the risers. Let your inspiration run wild here!

Staircase Basics

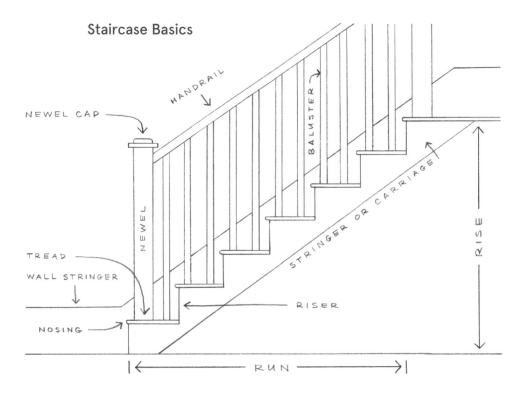

NEWEL CAP

HANDRAIL

BALUSTER

NEWEL

STRINGER OR CARRIAGE

TREAD

WALL STRINGER

RISER

RISE

NOSING

RUN

Jazzy's CHAPTER 4 CHECKLIST

☐ Do you feel like you could pick paint colors (or at least know where to start) if needed? Did you find a wall in your house that's asking for something EPIC?

☐ Were you honest about how you might use the floors in your house and how they need to fit your lifestyle?

☐ Have you started noticing floors when you're out and about? Coffee shops, subway stations, even the dentist's office? This shows you're thinking about floors!

If you answered "no" to any of the above, you have more work to do! If it's paint that's tripping you up, get a fresh set of eyes on your paint choices and ask a friend for their opinion. Still not sure about your floors? That's okay—it's normal! Spend more time out and about paying close attention to floors, and something will inevitably catch your eye.

5   EVERYTHING KITCHEN—
       THE HEART OF THE HOME

"I promise you'll love your kitchen and
you'll have a lot less gray hair when
it's all said and done."

The first kitchen I ever did was really tough. Not because I disliked my contractor or because I couldn't stick to a certain design (although that was hard!), but mostly because I had no idea what went into a kitchen. And I felt added pressure because it was my own house. There were *so many parts* and they all had to work together, which meant I had to have them figured out before I started. So, if you want to get a jump on designing a beautiful kitchen—whether you're building a brand new kitchen or renovating an existing one—I've put together a list I like to call the Everything Kitchen Checklist and I've added it to the back of this book. (See page 268.) This list might seem like a no-brainer, but I bet there's at least one thing on there you hadn't thought of. It took me years and literally hundreds of kitchens to compile this list. To say it's comprehensive is an understatement. The best way to use it is to go through and mark out anything that doesn't apply to your project and then fill in all the blanks for what's left. If you can fill in all those blanks before you start, I promise you'll love your kitchen and you'll have a lot less gray hair when it's all said and done. Oh, and one more thing: remember that pesky house story we identified in chapter 1? It's more important now than ever!

Kitchen Cabinets

The first thing you want to decide when you're choosing your cabinets is whether you want paint grade or stain grade cabinets. You guessed it: paint grade cabinets get painted and stain grade cabinets get stained. Paint grade cabinets are usually made of poplar or maple and can have more knots and imperfections that the paint will hide. However, the wood for stain grade cabinets—commonly made of white oak or walnut—will be "clear," meaning it has very few knots or imperfections and should take stain beautifully. Obviously, these are different kinds of wood, so if you stain paint grade cabinets, they probably won't look great, and if you paint stain grade cabinets, you're just wasting money.

Trust me.

Pro Tip: If you're not changing the layout of your kitchen, look into a cabinet refacing company that will change out only the doors. They'll reface your cabinets for a whole new look without having to rip out your entire kitchen. A major money saver!

Cabinet Styles

The second thing you have to decide is the door style. Each cabinet style—
Shaker, flat panel, plywood, or open shelving—will work with any of the four
core designs. It's the hardware you select that will truly ink your house story
into the design . . . more on that in a second.

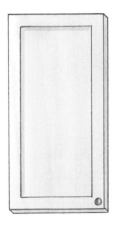

Shaker

Flat Panel

Plywood

Open Shelving

Jazzy's

FAVORITE KITCHEN-CABINET
PAINT COLORS

SHERWIN-WILLIAMS:
SW 6465 SPEARMINT

SHERWIN-WILLIAMS:
SW 7749 LAUREL WOODS

SHERWIN-WILLIAMS:
SW 7005 PURE WHITE

SHERWIN-WILLIAMS:
SW 9140 BLUSTERY SKY

SHERWIN-WILLIAMS:
SW 7645 THUNDER GRAY

SHERWIN-WILLIAMS:
SW 7067 CITYSCAPE

SHERWIN-WILLIAMS:
SW 6258 TRICORN BLACK

Choosing Your Cabinet Color

The third thing you have to decide when it comes to your cabinets is the color and whether they will be painted or stained. In addition to the paint grade versus stain grade distinction, there are two kinds of cabinets: custom cabinets and prefab cabinets. Prefab cabinets will have predetermined stain and paint colors—you'll look at a few different samples from the manufacturer and choose one. In my experience, if you're looking for a popular color (think white, gray, or black stain), prefab cabinetry is a great option! With custom cabinets, a cabinet maker will come to your home and make you samples based on the wood you've chosen.

If you don't know what the heck I'm talking about, that's okay! Have a chat with your carpenter or contractor, and they should be able to guide you in the right direction.

Cabinet Hardware

Now that you've nailed down your cabinet, pick a cabinet hardware that really speaks to your style so that your design is cohesive. This is the jewelry of the kitchen. Although I'm someone who is really bad at accessorizing myself (I honestly own, maybe, two necklaces), I can pick cabinet hardware with the best of 'em. So, where to start? First of all—do your cabinets need hardware? If your cabinets are super modern, or "flat panel," you might not need hardware and you can skip this part. Otherwise, chances are you'll need some handles or "pulls" and maybe some knobs to complete your kitchen. This is a great place to reference your house story and make it all come together.

CONTEMPORARY	COTTAGE	TRADITIONAL	RUSTIC

Maybe you're like me and your style is Traditional Cape Cod with Industrial accents. I chose paint grade, Shaker-style cabinets with a beadboard inset to make my cabinetry SUPER Cape Cod and Traditional. But then I added a more industrial pull with visible screws that have a pop of metal to set the tone and bring in the Industrial element of my style. My cabinets are, in a nutshell, exactly my house story.

I truly believe you should pick what makes you happy and what works best for your lifestyle, but I also think there are some specific hardware choices that drive home each core design in a big way.

HOW TO ORDER HARDWARE

1. Count your doors and drawers. You can use the same "pulls" on doors and drawers or you can use knobs on doors and pulls on drawers. Beware of any large drawers or appliances that might need bigger pulls and count accordingly.

2. Go online or in person to the store and purchase the number of each type based on your count. Once they arrive and your cabinets are installed, lay each piece of hardware in front of your cabinet doors/drawers to make sure you got it right.

3. Exchange/modify as needed, then start installing. This is best practice because once you drill into your cabinets, you really don't want to have to redo them. (Trust me, it's not fun!) Make sure you have every piece of hardware first, then start installing. Need tips on installing your own cabinet hardware? Flip to page 238.

Jazzy's FAVORITE PLACES TO SHOP FOR CABINET HARDWARE

Anthropologie	Restoration Hardware
Build.com	
Etsy	Schoolhouse Electric
Rejuvenation	
	World Market

Open Shelving

I love adding open shelving to my kitchen projects because it can bring so much depth and character to the space. Whether you're adding a single shelf next to the range or removing existing upper cabinetry to install a few rows of open shelves in its place, styling shelves is a fun and impactful way to carry through your house story. If you've got pretty plates and cups hiding behind cabinet doors, why not turn them into functional art pieces? And no, that doesn't include the kids' sippy cups (you can keep those stored safely behind a cabinet door and out of eyesight—ha!). Oh, and one more thing: styling open shelves isn't as easy as it looks—you can't just throw a bunch of stuff up there and expect it to make your eyes do a happy dance. But I've styled a lot of shelves in my day, so I have this down to a science and I'm here to help.

How to Style Open Shelves in Your Kitchen

1. **Group things in threes.** Start by gathering all of the things you'd like to display on your kitchen shelves: glassware, plates, bowls, a box of recipe cards, cutting boards, utensils in a crock, and so on. If you have four items you're styling with, try grouping three of them together in one cluster and the other item slightly away from the group of three. This arrangement would work with a stack of bowls, a crock of utensils, and a plant with a stack of plates slightly off to the side—you get the picture. Like items also look good grouped together. Maybe on one of your shelves you display all of your matching serveware, and your other shelves showcase a variety of items.

2. **Layer, layer, layer.** Use books to serve as a platform on which you can stack items, tuck things with varying heights behind and in front of the other and play around with depth. You'd be surprised how much of a difference it might make to move something 1 inch forward or 1 inch back. Experiment with it!

3. **Mix textures.** Your shelves could look one-dimensional and not very exciting if they're showcasing decor that all has the same finish or look. Make sure you work in something vintage or an organic texture, like wood, to add variety to the vignette (that's a fancy word for a group of stuff that's styled together). Adding something with a metal finish such as brass or copper is always a good call. Add something glass (think, water glasses), something old, and something natural.

4. **Put a plant on it.** My favorite rule. Plants bring so much life to kitchen shelves—even faux plants! Adding at least one plant to your open shelving will draw the eye to the shelves and add depth to your design. A trick for using faux plants: Pop one into a really pretty ceramic planter or basket, and it will look beautiful and REAL! And if you place your plants on higher shelves, no one will even notice the difference—and you're off the hook for watering them!

5. **Make it personal.** If you're thinking, "Wait, Jas, in my kitchen?" That's right. The kitchen might be my favorite place to add personal touches. Frame some photos and put them on the shelf. These don't have to be professional photos, a selfie from your phone is completely acceptable, and sometimes even preferred. If the photo makes you smile, it's perfect. Maybe you print them in black-and-white for a cleaner, more monochrome look. Art on kitchen shelves is unexpected and something every designer does, and you should do it too! The same goes for treasured keepsakes. Bring out those little mementos you grabbed on your last trip and let them shine!

QUICK SHELF-STYLING CHECKLIST

☐ Plants

☐ Varying materials

☐ Something glass

☐ Something brass

☐ Something vintage

☐ Something colorful

☐ A book or two

☐ Personal extras

Multiple glass colors add dimension.

Framed art is unexpected and a great convo-starter!

Wooden charger plates double as a back layer.

Woven wood blinds add texture.

A mirror reflects light back into the room.

Stacks of dishes are functional and add visual interest.

Don't forget plants!

Cutting boards add organic texture and get used regularly.

MORSE'S
EST. 1918
SAUERKRAUT

Countertop Materials

Once you choose your cabinets and hardware, it's time to choose your countertops. First off, there are two different ways to buy countertops: you can purchase slabs of material and have them custom fabricated, or you can choose a prefab kitchen countertop option. Prefab countertops come in set sizes and edge details and might make things easier for you, but you also might not have as many options to choose from.

When choosing a countertop material, it's important to consider how you live and not just pick what you think will look good. For example, quartz is a man-made material that not only looks great but is super durable. Granite has a different look, it is a natural material, and though it's not as indestructible as quartz, it's still very durable. Marble—we all know marble: it's the "Hey, come over here and see how pretty I am!" material—is most people's dream choice. And though it may have a beautiful look and is unique in that no two pieces are the same, if you live like the rest of us (think wine, tomato sauce, olive oil, friends with cups), marble will be your worst nightmare. Why? Because it stains and etches. Wood is also a beautiful choice for countertops and can bring a rustic vibe to your design. However, it can also be easy to damage with regular use and spills; so if you love wood, then consider using it on an island only. Once you decide how much you're willing to chase your friends around with coasters, choose your material, and then you can think about colors.

Countertop Finishes

  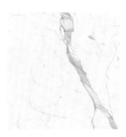 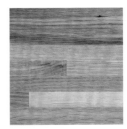

Quartz   Granite   Marble   Wood

Jazzy's

FAVORITE COUNTERTOP PICKS FOR
THE FOUR CORE DESIGNS

Contemporary: Quartz, polished finish, 2.5-inch square miter edge finish

Cottage: Black granite, leather finish, 1.25-inch square miter edge finish

Traditional: Marble, honed finish, ogee edge finish

Rustic: Wood, satin finish, 1.5-inch edge finish

Edge Finishes

Confession: I always use a flat edge finish for countertops, but there's a big world of edge finish options out there. If your core design is Traditional, you might find yourself drawn to a more detailed edge finish—so go for it! Talk to your contractor or countertop company about your edge finish options and what they'd recommend for your chosen material. If you've got resale in your future, your best bet is to keep it simple with a flat edge finish because it has the most mass appeal.

> *Pro Tip:* If you want to really *live* in your house (you know, with the red wine and the olive oil and the coffee stains), quartz or porcelain are super-durable materials, and they come in so many prints. Get the look of marble without all the fuss: win-win! If you've just got your heart set on the real thing, I've discovered the fountain of youth for marble: UV coating. There are specialized companies that will treat marble countertops with a UV finish that seals the marble, protecting it from damage. If this sounds cool to you, ask your contractor if they know of anyone in your area who can perform this service, and then you're golden!

Flat-Edge

Half-Bezel

Reverse-Bevel

¼ Bevel

Full-Bullnosed

Arris-Edge

Half-Bullnosed

Demi-Bullnosed

Ogee-Bullnosed

Waterfall-Edge

½ Top-Round

Ogee-Edge

Cove-Ogee

¼ Top-Bottom Round

Dupont-Edge

Cove-Edge

Backsplash

There are so many options when it comes to kitchen backsplash. There are the ever-popular subway tiles, penny round tiles, and mosaic tiles for days. There's a "self-splash" backsplash, which is when you use the same material as your countertop for the backsplash, making it one continuous piece running up the wall. This self-splash can be anything from 2 inches to a full slab (this is what I have in my own house). I've even used wallpaper as a backsplash.

So, where does someone begin when it's time to choose? Well, that's easy! Go back to your house story from chapter 1, think about how much you use your kitchen (if you're flinging water everywhere, wallpaper backsplash isn't for you), and then hit the interwebs to find some inspiration photos. Or even take this book into your local tile showroom or hardware store and pick a material that matches one of the photos. There isn't a right or wrong backsplash, as long as it's functional (that is, doesn't allow water to get to the drywall behind the countertop and drip down behind) and as long as it doesn't completely clash with the countertop. When in doubt, less is more. Keep it neutral and you won't regret it!

Jazzy's FAVORITE PLACES TO SHOP FOR BACKSPLASH TILE

Clé Tile

Floor & Decor

Hardware stores, such as Home Depot or Lowe's

Local tile showrooms

Zia Tile

Tile Layouts

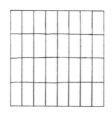

Vertical Stacked

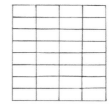

Horizontal Stacked

Running Bond

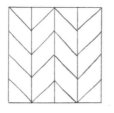

Chevron

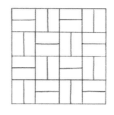

Basket Weave

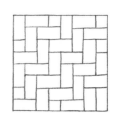

Herringbone

15 FUN BACKSPLASH IDEAS

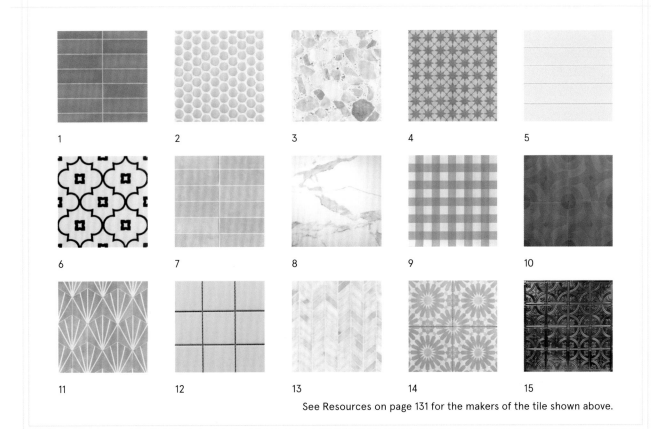

1
2
3
4
5
6
7
8
9
10
11
12
13
14
15

See Resources on page 131 for the makers of the tile shown above.

My first rule of thumb when it comes to picking a backsplash is to wait until you've chosen your cabinet style, hardware, cabinet color, and your countertops. By the time you've made those decisions, you'll know if your backsplash should be more neutral and minimal or if it can be a place to showcase some color and pattern. For example, if a client of mine wants dark green cabinets and a marble countertop, I know that a busy backsplash material might look like there's too much going on in one space. I'd install some white subway tile or self-splash marble for a seamless look. But if a client has their heart set on white Shaker cabinets and dark gray quartz countertops, I know I can choose something bolder for the backsplash. Maybe I'd install hand-painted or hand-crafted tiles in a blueish hue. Make sense?

If you're still stumped or unsure if your materials go well together, let's make this easy. Scroll through Pinterest and Instagram, leaf through design books and magazines, and flag your favorite kitchens. Once you narrow down the photo you like the most—and the style that will work best within your house story and the way you live—copy it! Imitation is the sincerest form of flattery, right?

Three FOOLPROOF BACKSPLASH AND COUNTERTOP COMBOS THAT WORK WITH ANY CORE DESIGN

- Subway tile backsplash + Carrera marble countertops

- Penny round tile backsplash + white quartz countertops

- Self-splash—same material for the countertops and backsplash

Pro tip: Hire a pro! For real though, don't DIY your backsplash. Sure, we make it look easy on TV, and there are a million how-to videos you can watch online. But at the end of the day, I think it's totally worthwhile to pay somebody to do the work. If you don't install tile regularly, it's hard to keep your tile from becoming crooked as you install it. Chances are, you don't already own all the supplies you'd need to install your backsplash, so you'd have to buy a bunch of tools, and by the time you buy all those tools—and spend three months trying to lay your tile level—you could have just hired somebody who could do it in a day. Trust me.

Grout

If you need to pick a grout for your tile, I've got some tips. See page 175 for a thorough grout explanation.

Appliances

Before you hit the stores, let's talk about gas versus electric appliances. If you're doing a renovation, the easiest and least expensive upgrade is going to be to stay the same. Gas to gas, electric to electric. This may seem like a no-brainer, but let's talk through it. If you already have electric, all you'll do is unplug your existing range and exchange it for a new, similar size range. If you already have gas, the same applies. Pretty simple stuff.

However, if you want to switch from electric to gas, which is a common upgrade that most of my clients are interested in, it's not always as easy as you think. Make sure you have a conversation with your contractor BEFORE you go and buy a gas range. If you're pining for a gas range and oven, I need you to come down to Earth with me for a second. Running a gas line is often not easy. Some houses don't have gas at all, some houses have gas only at the fireplaces (think about how far away your fireplace is from your kitchen), and the foundation and attic space in your house will also affect how easy it is to relocate the gas line. This could be an easy fix, or it could be a big expensive problem.

This is also a great time to consider how you use your kitchen. Would you prefer to have double ovens? Would you prefer to have a cooktop with your oven located elsewhere? Do you need a microwave? Are you going to build in the microwave? Are you a baker? Are you a BBQ extraordinaire? Answering all of these questions will help you not just to buy some appliances but to pick out appliances that can really serve your family. Discuss all these things with your contractor or appliance salesperson, and they should be able to help you find the perfect appliances.

Pro Tip: Don't try to DIY your own gas line if you want to switch from electric. Make sure a pro helps you figure out if the switch is possible in the first place and pay them to do the job. Hire a pro and never mess with gas!

Appliance Finishes

Appliances come in all different finishes. The most common finishes are stainless or white. There are also black stainless, matte black, and colorful retro appliances. Although I'm intrigued by these other options, the majority of the projects I do have a matching set of stainless-steel appliances, and they just kind of disappear into the design. They're beautiful, but I'm not making a statement with them. Once in a while I'll get crazy and use a white refrigerator or a stainless black set of appliances, but most of the time, a nice matching set of stainless-steel appliances is perfect. If you're considering resale, this is probably the smartest move.

Stainless   Black   White   Retro

Best practice: Buy an appliance suite. That means buy all of your appliances from the same brand so they match. If you can avoid it, don't buy the fridge that's on sale, the oven that's on sale, the microwave that's on sale, the dishwasher that's on sale . . . should I keep going? If you grab all those bargain buys and they're all made by different manufacturers, they're going to look disjointed as a set. They'll have different stainless finishes, different handles, different logos, and different colored lights on the clock and display.

Speaking of appliances, not all refrigerators are created equal. There are full-depth refrigerators and counter-depth refrigerators. Make sure you discuss with your contractor the depth of your cabinetry and the opening for your refrigerator before purchasing. All of this to say, you need to know the dimensions of all of your appliances, including the hood, dishwasher, microwave, range, ovens, and refrigerator, BEFORE you start building your cabinetry.

Pro Tip: Have a hankering for a vintage-inspired refrigerator? Maybe you don't choose one for your main refrigerator because it's not as functional, but you can have some fun with that retro feel in another location. Think about adding a cute little vintage-inspired fridge to your bar, game room, bonus room, or home gym. Cheers!

Hoods

Okay, now that you've figured out your range, cooktop, oven—electric or gas, whatever configuration you decided to go with—it's time to talk about hoods. A vent above a cooktop is not only a nice amenity, but it's also a necessity: by code, you need to have a vent above your cooktop in all renovations. Making sure you determine what type of hood you want is key in your kitchen planning, because you'll need to know the size before your cabinets are built. Adding one after the fact is a pain!

Chimney

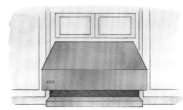

Under cabinet

Micro

Custom

Another conversation to have with your contractor is if there isn't already a hood in your kitchen, what will it take to add a vented hood? Sometimes it's not an option. If it's not an option, talk to your contractor about charcoal filters or what else you can use.

And let's say you'd like to replace the microwave with a hood: there are ductless and non-ductless options. Chances are your microwave is ductless, meaning it doesn't vent outside. There are still some options that might be better than a microwave, but for the most part you're going to want to add a duct. Add this to your things-to-talk-to-my-contractor-about list!

Lighting

Congrats! Your kitchen is almost done, but now there's one more thing: the lighting. Lighting is something that, in my opinion, can make or break a kitchen. Your cabinets, hardware, and backsplash can be on point, you can have the perfect appliances—but it could all feel a little lackluster with the wrong lighting. So don't mess it up!

Before you even think about ordering lighting, look around at your kitchen. Go ahead, I'll wait. Do you have a lot of natural light? Do you have a lot of windows? Is the space well lit to begin with, or could it be brighter? Is your kitchen closed off or open to the rest of the house? What lights would you keep? What lights would you replace? Do you have a good understanding of how light works in your kitchen, and what would make it better? Good, let's move on.

Most kitchens you see will have some sort of lighting that hangs above the island or above a kitchen sink—they're called pendants. Pendants can do wonders for a kitchen in terms of adding a "wow" factor, and they can make a space feel more finished. They can also help drive home your style. But before you hang anything, you should determine if it's going to make your space too busy. For example, if you have an open concept space and your dining room is right next to your kitchen, there could be too many hanging lights in view if your dining room also has some pendants or a chandelier. If other rooms are visible from the kitchen, look around from all different angles to see how the pendants would play off the rest of your home's design.

If you don't have an island, or pendants hanging over the island aren't the best bet for your space, I suggest hanging a pendant over the sink and installing can lights or flush-mount lights over the island instead.

LIGHTING VOCABULARY

Can lights: You probably have can lights, also known as recessed lights, in your kitchen right now. They're lightbulbs housed in a metal can that's set into and flush with the ceiling.

Flush mount: A light fixture that is affixed directly to the ceiling.

Pendant: A light that is suspended from the ceiling by a chain, cord, rope, and so on.

Sconce: A sconce light is a light fixture that's installed on a wall. Depending on the light, it can point upward or downward.

| CONTEMPORARY | COTTAGE | TRADITIONAL | RUSTIC |

Little Changes with Big Impact

Want to work with what's already there? Consider can-light conversion kits, where you change one or two of your existing can lights to pendants or flush-mount options. Talk to your contractor or use a DIY conversion kit. Either way this is a pretty minor change with a big impact.

Used to be a can light!

Can Lights and Cabinets

If you have can lights in your kitchen ceiling that you want to move or you're installing fresh can lights, you'll want to think about the distance of the lights to your cabinets or open shelves.

There are two schools of thought on how far away you should place the can lights. The first is when you're standing at your countertop facing your cabinets, chopping on a cutting board, the light should hit your hands. Which means that your lights are close to your cabinets. The second school of thought is that though it may be annoying to have light behind your head (making your head a shadow over your countertop), it lights up the pathway between your island and your cabinetry better. And when you open your cabinet, the cabinet door doesn't cut the light, which can be distracting. Okay, okay, this might all be a little too nerdy for most people, but I think it's important for you to know there's a method behind the madness.

So, what's the answer, Jas? I like to put my lights farther away from the cabinets because I feel like it makes the whole room brighter, not just the perimeters. But I also like to install undercabinet lighting (not fluorescent!) to light the backsplash. So go ahead, get in your kitchen, and pretend to chop up veggies on a cutting board. That's right—I want to see chopped veggies on a cutting board! *Wow, those imaginary knife cuts are perfect.* Can you clearly see what you're doing? Would you mind light behind your head? Great! Now pick a school of thought and convey that light placement to your contractor.

Pro Tip: If you're not going to install undercabinet lighting, move the can lights a little closer to the cabinets and they will brighten up your countertops and backsplash.

NIX THE FLUORESCENTS

Got the fluorescent light blues? There's never a good time to have a fluorescent light in the kitchen. No matter what, if you do nothing else, have your contractor take out fluorescent lighting.

Running a Whip (Secret Pro-Talk Stuff)

If you're lucky enough to be doing new construction or a major remodel, chances are, during construction, your contractor's going to ask where you want your pendant lights, fans, a chandelier, or any other kind of lighting or ceiling fixtures. Let's be honest—if your kitchen is an empty shell without cabinets yet or too unfinished for you to even visualize the end (*when will construction be over?!*), figuring out where you want to hang a pendant light can feel like shooting a free-throw while blindfolded.

So if you have no idea where to put your lights yet, no sweat. Tell your contractor, "Let's run a whip," and then try not to be obvious with how cool that makes you feel. Running a whip means running a wire to the general location the lights will be and not actually cutting into the drywall until the rest of the construction is done. So, you can take a little more time to locate exactly where you want the lights. That way, you don't have to commit as early. Once your island is in place and your countertops are in, you can actually visualize your kitchen, and it's much easier to decide where you want your pendant lights, chandelier, ceiling fan, or can lights at that point.

Matching Finishes and Mixing Metals

I get asked all the time: Do I need to match my lighting, plumbing fixtures, and cabinet hardware? Unhelpful answer: It depends. Helpful answer: It's okay to mix and match! I like to pick two finishes and stick to those, but there are always exceptions to the rules. Take my kitchen, for example. I have black doorknobs, a chrome faucet, stainless appliances, chrome cabinet hardware, and antique brass pendant lights above my island. They all work together to accomplish my Traditional Cape Cod with Industrial accents style. In my opinion, though, even one more metal finish in this room would be TOO MUCH! My best advice: If you want to feel like you "have the eye" and make really informed decisions, find a photo of a kitchen online and try to match what you see. That's what I do! If you love a kitchen, just follow the finishes used in your inspiration photo and you won't regret it. And one more thing—if you're using brass, be aware of subtle differences in the finishes. Not all brass finishes are created equal, and if they aren't the same or really similar, you'll suddenly have five shades of brass competing in what you thought was going to be a really refined kitchen design.

TIPS FOR RESALE VALUE

If you're remodeling your kitchen in order to get top dollar for your home, or you know you'll eventually sell your home down the road, keep these tips in mind.

- Don't choose a backsplash that's too busy. Buyers will want to see themselves in the house and imagine their own style working in the space. A simple subway tile, self-splash, or penny round tiles are all classic and versatile options.

- As a general rule, aim for neutral colors. A bold color—for example, bright blue cabinets—won't appeal to everyone.

- If you can swing it, purchase all stainless-steel appliances. This is almost always a big selling point for buyers.

- If you're debating whether or not to add an island to your kitchen and you're going to sell your home in the future, add one (if it's in your budget). This will greatly increase the value of the home.

- Nix the fluorescents! If there are any fluorescent lights in your kitchen, get them outta there.

- Choose lighting that looks new and updated but isn't too trendy or style specific. Glass orb pendants or even lighting with a matte black metal finish would work beautifully. Brass, while very popular, can still turn off buyers because it's trendier.

CONTEMPORARY

Before

CONTEMPORARY ORGANIC MIDMODERN

KITCHEN

White Subway-
Tile Backsplash

Leather Stools at
Breakfast Bar

Lower Cabinets
Painted "Extra
White" by
Sherwin-Williams

Chimney-
Style Hood

Oversize Basket
Pendant Lighting

Quartz Marble-
Look Countertops

Stainless Appliances

Pull-Down
Faucet

Open Shelving with
Brass Brackets

After

Skip ahead to page 259 to see mood boards for the rest of the house!

TRADITIONAL

Before

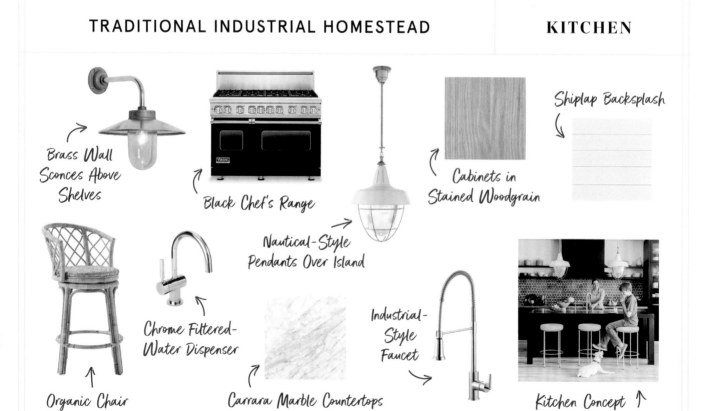

TRADITIONAL INDUSTRIAL HOMESTEAD

KITCHEN

Brass Wall Sconces Above Shelves

Black Chef's Range

Nautical-Style Pendants Over Island

Cabinets in Stained Woodgrain

Shiplap Backsplash

Organic Chair

Chrome Filtered-Water Dispenser

Carrara Marble Countertops

Industrial-Style Faucet

Kitchen Concept ↑

After

Skip ahead to page 265 to see mood boards for the rest of the house!

Jazzy's CHAPTER 5 CHECKLIST

☐ Did you start by creating a checklist of all the things you need to figure out for your own project? (I don't want you to forget anything—I got you!)

☐ Do you understand all the different pieces that have to work together to make your kitchen design work?

☐ Is your house story front and center in your decision making?

If you answered "no" to any of the above, you have more work to do!

6   IT'S NOT JUST A BATHROOM—LOOKING AT THE LOO

"This is the one room in our home where we are reminded to stop what we're doing and care for ourselves."

It's easy to forget about the bathroom, but really, it's one of the most important rooms—if not *the* most important—in the house. This is the one room in our home where we are reminded to stop what we're doing and care for ourselves. No matter how hectic our days, we start our mornings and end our evenings in the bathroom. And whether you have a twelve-step skincare routine (spoiler alert: I don't!), are a bubble-bath lover, or are more of a quick shower, brush your teeth, and run out the door kind of person, you still end up here. For a place with such a high responsibility—to help us care for ourselves—it better be pretty darn serene!

If you're looking around your bathroom and it doesn't feel like the lovely, welcoming escape of your dreams, don't sweat it. The good news is bathrooms are easy to update. Whether you're designing a new house and feel overwhelmed with the thought of picking everything for three new bathrooms (you poor thing!) or completely stuck with your ugly 1991 rental bathroom, there's a way to make your bathroom the happiest room in the house. Let's get to it!

Getting Started

The bathroom is connected to the rest of your house, and don't you forget it! When a friend of mine recently sent me a photo of his bathroom, asking what he should do with it, I immediately asked for photos of the outside of the house, the kitchen, and the living and dining rooms. He thought I was crazy, but I explained that your home design should be holistic, and your bathroom is a part of your house—not separate. The bathroom is one of the best places to add a *huge dose* of your personal style to your home and take your house story to the next level. Also, if you ignore your style and just go "rogue" on the bathroom design, your bathroom will feel like an outcast—and we certainly don't want that! So, stick with your style and whether you're buying new towels or a whole room of bathroom tile, you won't be disappointed.

Remember when I told you about the Everything Kitchen Checklist back in chapter 5? Remember how helpful it was to be able to go through and mark everything you'd need to figure out to update your space? Well, you guessed it, I've created an Everything Bathroom Checklist so you can make sure nothing gets overlooked for your project. I told you, I've got your back. (See page 269 for the Everything Bathroom Checklist.)

Once you've started that list and checked everything twice, the next step is to figure out what you can do with your bathroom. Let's talk layout. . . .

Bathroom Layout

The first and most important thing to look at in your bathroom is layout. Clients ask me all the time, "Can I switch my shower and toilet around?" "Can I make my built-in tub into a freestanding one?" "Can I make my single vanity into a double?" Oftentimes the answer is yes, but let's be honest—these are BIG undertakings, and when you're asking these questions, it's time to call a contractor. Changing the layout of your bathroom can make all the difference. But before you start ripping apart your house, make sure to ask yourself *why*. Is this change going to make the bathroom work better for your family? Is it going to increase the resale value? Is it worth spending the money? Remember, changing a floor plan just to change it is never the right option, and the cost of these changes add up quickly when it comes to your bathroom budget. Still think you want to change your floor plan? Cool! Here are some things to consider before chatting with your contractor.

Getting rid of the tub all together. I'm seeing a trend right now where a lot of my clients want just showers. That might work for your family, but it's a huge gamble when it comes to resale value. There are still a *lot* of people who won't buy a house if there isn't a tub in the primary bathroom. So, if you can fit them both, I would recommend leaving the tub.

Double vanities are GREAT, but make sure you have the room. If you don't, stick with a single vanity and enough counter space to get ready properly. Don't try to make something work that just doesn't.

Separate the toilet room. If there's any way you can swing it, I would highly recommend getting your toilet into its own little "toilet room" (think pocket or barn door). This is something you will never regret because it will make your bathroom function much better, and it's *great* for resale value. #privacy

Now that you know what you need to update in your bathroom and you've considered the layout, let's talk about all the different pieces that make a bathroom. These will apply to every bathroom, from a bathroom undergoing construction to a bathroom that just needs a cosmetic refresh. You might be surprised how many things there are to consider! These are the details we can't get to on television but that stump homeowners in real life. They also make all the difference when you're seeing the space in person and not just on the screen.

Sinks and Vanities

There's so much more to a sink and vanity than just brushing your teeth! The vanity and sink in a bathroom aren't only necessary, these components are also a great opportunity to add a whole lotta style from your house story. Before you even set foot in a store or start looking on the interwebs, make sure you know your measurements. Then get ready because there are so many options out there!

TYPE: Undermount Cabinet
STYLE: Timeless

TYPE: Vessel Sink
STYLE: Modern

TYPE: Pedistal Sink
STYLE: Traditional

TYPE: Freestanding Vanity
STYLE: Timeless

TYPE: Furniture
STYLE: Vintage

TYPE: Wall Mount
STYLE: Modern

In order to make your sink/vanity combo work with your house story, you should mix and match! If you have a powder room (this is a bathroom that has no shower or bathtub, just a toilet and sink), your vanity choice is really important. Why? Because this is essentially the sole piece in the room that will define and showcase your style. Say your design is Modern Craftsman. A vessel sink on a freestanding console might be the perfect way to go. However, there aren't rules as to what you use as a sink or vanity! One of my favorite things to do is find old pieces of furniture, sewing tables, even metal pedestals and use them as my vanities. Sometimes adding a fresh, modern sink to a vintage table with chippy paint is the perfect pairing of old and new that cements your design.

And when it comes to sinks, you can get creative as well. I've even used an old birdbath and drilled a hole in the bottom. Maybe your style is Contemporary Organic. Adding earthy wooden or leather pulls to a vanity with sleek, flat panel cabinetry would accomplish both parts of your design. The idea is not to feel like you have to keep everything so one-note by following only one design style. Take all aspects of your house story into account and see where you can let each part shine in harmony. Think outside the box!

If your sink and vanity are existing and can't be changed, don't despair. The easiest update is to change out the hardware on the doors and drawers. This can make a huge difference. The next easiest fix is to paint or stain the vanity. And if you want to take it even one step further, you can switch out the vanity countertop and faucet.

Jazzy's FAVORITE BATHROOM COUNTERTOPS

RUGGED CONCRETE QUARTZ BY CAESARSTONE

MANIFICA ENCORE PORCELAIN SLAB IN
HONED ARABESCATO GREY BY BEDROSIANS

PATINATED COPPER MADE BY A LOCAL ARTISAN

Fixtures

Have you ever walked into a bathroom and seen a really cool faucet coming out of the wall and wondered how it got there? Well, that could be *your* faucet! With a little bit of planning and know-how, it's possible to think of a faucet as being so much more than the thing that pumps out water. Using a faucet to complement your sink and vanity is a no-brainer, but using a faucet with some style . . . now we're talking!

FIXTURES VOCABULARY

When shopping for bathroom faucets, it's important that you know exactly what kind of plumbing holes you're dealing with on your countertop. This mostly applies to updating an existing bathroom—if you're building your bathroom concept from scratch, you can choose whatever you please!

Bridge: Many faucets require three holes for installation, but most bridge faucets only need two. These faucets are taller in size and "bridge" the hot and cold handles and spout off of two pieces below that mount into the countertop. If you have three holes in your countertop, some bridge faucets are made to accommodate that plumbing setup with a deck plate.

Single hole: A single-hole faucet wraps the spout and hot and cold water controls all into one mechanism, so it only needs one hole for plumbing through the countertop. This can be a really seamless, clean look and also improves functionality because you can adjust your temperature easier.

Wall mount: A wall-mount faucet is exactly as you've probably guessed— it's a waterspout and hot and cold handles mounted to the wall instead of the countertop. These either can be widespread mounts or have all features combined in one piece.

Widespread mount: A widespread mount involves a spout and hot and cold handles that are all mounted separately from one another on the countertop. Installing a widespread mount requires three holes.

Faucet Finishes

Once you've chosen the shape of your faucet, you still need to choose the finish. Chrome, brushed stainless, brass, oil-rubbed bronze, black . . . there are so many options when it comes to finishes, but I would recommend having your faucet match your showerhead, tub filler, drains, and so on. Pick one finish and stick with it!

Jazzy's FAVORITE BATHROOM FAUCETS

KOHLER PURIST WIDESPREAD CROSS HANDLE, CHROME

KOHLER BRIDGE FAUCET, BRASS

KOHLER SINGLE-HOLE FAUCET, BLACK

Bathtubs and Showers

So, if you aren't already overwhelmed, get ready, because you're about to be. The options for bathtubs and showers are endless, and it's really easy to get lost. But don't give in! Measure your space, know what you want, stick to your house story—and don't give up!

Bathtub Options

Drop in: Used in a more traditional style, a drop-in tub is the perfect option if you want to have somewhere to sit outside of the tub. By having a "deck" around the top, this tub layout gives lots of options for style, sizes, and shapes.

Integrated: Easier to use in smaller bathrooms, these tubs work as a tub/shower combo and are a sleek option. Usually made of fiberglass or cast iron, it's *super* important to get the measurement right. *Please note:* You order these tubs with the drain on the left or the right. There's nothing worse than getting the tub inside the bathroom only to find out your plumbing is on the wrong side. It's happened to me!

Freestanding: Talk about a dream tub! Freestanding tubs can be modern, sleek, vintage, or rustic—it just depends on the material. When it comes to freestanding tubs, the tub does the talking, along with the tub filler. Be warned, though, most freestanding tubs don't have some of the amenities (think jets, bubbles, aromatherapy, and so on) that drop-in tubs have—so what you gain in style you might lose in comfort or bells and whistles.

Shower Options

Okay, so you've figured out your bathtub. What about your shower? If your bath and shower are together, you've already fought half the battle! But if your shower is separate from your bathtub, you have more work to do. And if you thought there was a lot that went into choosing your bathtub, the shower's even more intense! If you've already picked your vanity faucet (style and finish), I would recommend using the coordinating pieces in your shower. See, that's one thing off your list already! Oh, but don't forget the handshower, rainhead, or any sort of steam shower you might want to add. Your contractor needs to know about these from Day 1, so think about how you're going to use your shower (my clients with kids and dogs love their handshowers) and pick accordingly.

> *Pro Tip:* Not all shower glass is created equal. Glass naturally has a blue/green hue, so if you don't want to see your shower tile through that color spectrum, you need to order Starphire glass, which has much less blue/green.

Bathroom Tile

The world of tile is constantly changing, and because of the magnitude of styles, formats, colors, materials—you name it—the options are truly endless. Whether you're shopping for tile online or in person, it seems there's a spiffy new option each week. But don't let that intimidate you. It's never a bad thing to have too many options, I say! That being said, there are some general tips and points to be made about the best tile options for a bathroom, and how to choose what's right for your own home. So, let's get to learning, shall we?

First of all, there isn't a right or wrong tile to use in your bathroom from a design perspective (this is all personal preference), but there is a right or wrong tile choice when it comes to functionality. The bathroom is wet, meaning there's water on the floor, so you need a tile that's "wet rated" or confirmation from the manufacturer that it's suitable for wet areas, and also going to have enough grip so you're not sliding all over the place! Not all tile works in a bathroom—there's also a big difference between bathroom floor tile and wall tile—so make sure you're looking for this designation when purchasing. Okay, now that I got my annoying mom warnings out of the way (I'm a mom now, I can do that!), let's talk about how FUN tile can be.

PROS AND CONS OF FLOORING TYPES

You could really get lost in the sea of tile options when trying to decide what shape you want. Subway, hexagonal, square—they even make tile that looks like mermaid or fish scales when installed. But before you dive into all the shape options, it's easier to decide first if you want large format, mosaic, or mini mosaic tile. Depending on the look you want, you might just be able to find the vibe you're after in any of those three forms. This is another one of those times I'm going to urge you to hop on your laptop or phone and look to Pinterest and design blogs to get inspiration for your space. Pay attention to other cool bathrooms you see in person—do you like tiles that are larger or smaller? Shiny or more matte? Do you like a clean, classic look, or are you aiming to make a statement? And remember, you'll need to consider where this tile is going and how the type of tile will work in that situation. Wall tiles are different than floor tiles, so make sure you check the product details before you fall in love with a certain look.

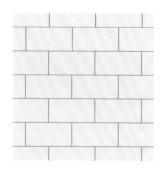

PORCELAIN

Pros

Not porous

Durable

Available in many styles

Uniform in look

Affordable to install

No maintenance required

Cons

Machine-made, so may have less character

Fragile before installation

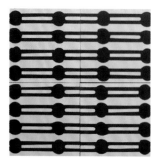

CEMENT

Pros

Handcrafted and unique

Has a stylish matte finish

Affordable

Cons

Porous

Thick and heavy

Installation is expensive

Maintenance is required to reseal regularly

Irregular grout lines

WOOD LOOK

Pros

Get the organic texture of wood without the upkeep

No maintenance required

Easy to install

Printed, so you don't have the irregularity of real wood

Doesn't shrink and swell like real wood

Affordable

Cons

Can only be used on flat floors that don't require bullnose, stair, or edge pieces

Could clash with other real wood flooring in your home

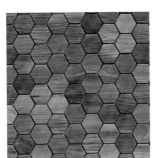

TEAK

Pros

Beautiful

Long-lasting

Adds an organic element

Cons

Requires regular oiling and maintenance

Boards could gap and pop as wood shrinks and swells

Material and installation are expensive

HANDCRAFTED

Pros

Beautiful and unique

Affordable to install

Maintenance is minimal

Cons

Not suitable for floors

Material is expensive

Irregular grout lines

How to Shop for Tile

My friends and family ask me all the time how they should find tile for their houses. Whether you're shopping for tile in person or online, you need to be prepared with measurements, samples, and a good eye.

IN PERSON   Selecting tile in person is my favorite way to find the best tile. I recommend going to your local tile showroom and bringing the following: wood floor samples, cabinet samples, paint chips, hardware samples, and photos of your bathroom. The photos you bring are really important! The designer or salesperson can only help you with the information you give them, so the more photos you show them, the better! My trick when taking photos is to use the "corner to corner" method, meaning you take at least four photos (one from each corner) of each room.

ONLINE   Sometimes, the only option for shopping is online, and I totally get that. If you're ordering tile from a website, my recommendation is to order a sample of a few different tiles you're thinking of and wait to decide until you see the tile in person. If this absolutely isn't an option, I'd recommend ordering your bathroom tile in stages so you can at least see the different tile elements as they come in and build off of them. For example, buy your floor tile first. Once you have that in your hot little hands (and realize it's a different shade in real life than it was on the computer screen), you can pick wall tile that goes with it. Make sense?

HOW TO MEASURE FOR TILE

Tile is measured by the square foot. Measure two sides of the room in inches, multiply them together, then divide by 144. Your answer is how many square feet of tile you'll need. When it comes time to buy, always order 15 to 20 percent more tile than your actual measurement calls for. This will allow you (or your installer) to account for cuts and broken tile pieces.

Jazzy's FAVORITE BATHROOM TILE

SCALLOPED CEMENT
FLOOR TILES

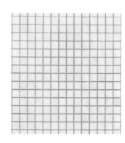

THASSOS WHITE MARBLE
MINI MOSAIC SHOWER PAN

ZELLIGE WALL TILE

WHAT THE GROUT?

Okay, if you're like me, when you did your first bathroom, you had
NO CLUE what grout was. Or maybe you're learning about it this very
moment. Either way, I'm not judging. Anyway, grout is my best friend now,
and I think it can be yours as well. Whether you're DIYing your bathroom
or working with a contractor, the time will come to finish the tile and you
will be asked, "What grout color do you want?" Grout is what's between
the tile. It's the final step and it's an important one, not just functionally
(think waterproofing) but also from a design standpoint. The best thing to
do is ask your contractor or local tile shop for a "grout chart," which will
give you lots of color options to choose from. That said, never blindly pick
grout! Always put the grout sample next to the tile to see how it looks.
And remember, all shades of white are different, so this is especially
important if you're trying to pick white grout for white subway tile. At the
end of the day, there are two options with grout. You either match the
tile (my trick is to blur my eyes, and if it "disappears," it's a good match)
or contrast the tile (think white tile with dark gray grout). The best way
to choose which option to go with is to go back to your house story and
bathroom inspiration photos. Good luck!

Resale Value

What you choose matters! So, in addition to sticking to your personal style, there's one more thing to keep in mind when picking through all the options for your bathroom, and it's B-O-R-I-N-G but oh so important . . . RESALE VALUE. That's right, you have to (well, I guess you don't *have to*, but don't come crying to me when you can't sell your home for top dollar) pick materials that are timeless and will work for you as well as for the next owner(s) of your home. I'm forever reminding my clients about resale value, and I'm forever getting dirty looks—but I don't care! When it comes to resale value, there are few important things to consider.

Quality: The quality of your bathroom materials is really important. This is a part of the house that gets used, and if your materials are shoddy, it will be evident. I'm all about using well-known brands, but that doesn't necessarily mean breaking the bank. If you find a material you like but haven't heard of the brand, do your research, read reviews, and make sure it's tried and tested. You can still score on saving by using reputable brands. And once you make your purchase, keep records of everything you buy, and *always* use a licensed contractor who pulls permits.

Trends: We've all seen it—the bathroom style that was hot for six months and then went out of style. Before you put something in your bathroom (at least something permanent; knock yourself out with cute towels, mats, shower curtains, and wallpaper!), ask if it's something you would want for the rest of your life. If the answer is no, maybe go in a different direction.

Perception: Sometimes, perception is reality. What I mean by this is you don't have to give up functionality or budget just because of resale value. If you don't have Calacatta marble (a timeless material, in my opinion) in your budget, go ahead and use really good porcelain tile that is printed to look like marble. It will wear beautifully and be great for resale.

Lighting, Mirrors, and Everything Fun!

Finally! You can really let your hair down and have some FUN with these things in your bathroom design. Yay! Truth be told—but not to scare you—the bathroom is pretty permanent, meaning that most of the things you put into your bathroom will be there for the next fifteen years (at least). But all is not lost, and the best way to personalize the bathroom is through all the accessories. And trust me, you'll know when you find the right piece that makes you super happy—and then instantly question your life because you're *way* too excited about a toilet-paper holder.

Lighting

Although you can definitely splurge on lighting without flinching, it's also not necessary. Lighting is one of the most important decisions in your bathroom. Where to start? Think about your house story! If you've already nailed part of your style with the vanity or tile, go ahead and use lighting to seal the deal. For example, if your style is Midcentury bungalow, you might have a really cute navy blue Craftsman-style vanity with a white quartz countertop that feels like a bungalow, and you can use the lighting and cabinet hardware to bring the Midcentury part of the design together. Perfect!

There aren't any rules for bathroom lighting other than you must consider using wet- or damp-rated lights close to areas where condensation will build up. If you're not sure how close a light fixture needs to be to a water source to qualify it as needing to be wet-rated, ask a professional—this can even be someone working at your local hardware store. Trust me on this; you don't want to mix water with electrical, people.

CONTEMPORARY	COTTAGE	TRADITIONAL	RUSTIC

Oh, and one more thing—the bathroom isn't the spot for "mood lighting." Because let's be honest, we all need those bright lights to find weird hairs growing from the tops of our ears. Gross but true!

Mirrors

Not only are there *endless* options for mirrors, they're an awesome way to add something a little "extra" to your bathroom. I'm not saying that everyone needs a statement mirror, but I do want to let you know, whether your mirror is "loud and proud" or "just there," it's still making a statement. So be intentional with your mirror choice and you won't regret it. My favorite part of the bathroom!

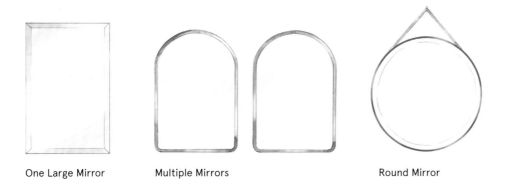

One Large Mirror   Multiple Mirrors   Round Mirror

Picking a Mirror

Remember your house story from chapter 1? Well, if you haven't already done it, a mirror is the perfect way to add your own unique style to your bathroom. Even if you only change out the mirror in your rental bathroom, you can still make a big impact! Mirrors range from very inexpensive to family heirloom prices, so set a budget and then start hunting!

Jazzy's FAVORITE PLACES TO SHOP FOR MIRRORS

Anthropologie   Vintage markets

CB2   West Elm

Pottery Barn   Yard sales

FAVE SHOWER CURTAINS

  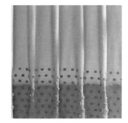

Saturated color can make a cold bathroom feel warm and welcoming.

A nod to the outdoors, prints with natural elements feel great in a bathroom.

Sometimes a little texture is all you need. Here, these poms steal the show.

FAVE WALLPAPERS

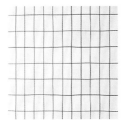  

Geometric pattern works great with modern or traditional design styles.

Neutral grass cloth can pair nicely with most design styles.

Do you have a smaller bathroom? Here's your permission to GO BOLD.

FAVE HAND TOWELS

And yes, a simple towel is just fine to add a soft pop of color.

If nothing else— textured hand towels!

Tassels can add a bit of sweetness to your bathroom.

And don't forget the bathmat!

VINTAGE

Before

Now that you've considered all these options, gather them together and make your own design board. This could be as easy as using Pinterest to create your own personal design inspo collage!

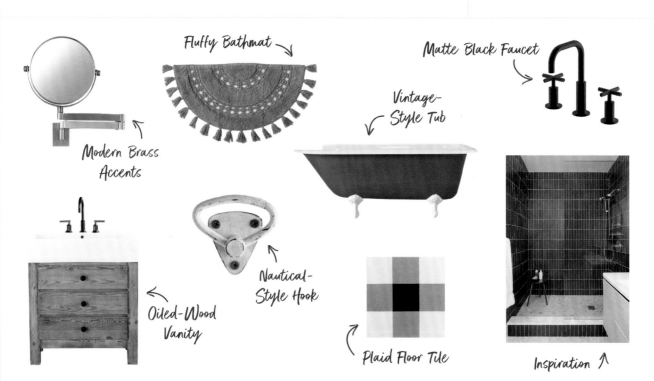

VINTAGE CRAFTSMAN COTTAGE

BATHROOM

Fluffy Bathmat

Matte Black Faucet

Modern Brass Accents

Vintage-Style Tub

Nautical-Style Hook

Oiled-Wood Vanity

Plaid Floor Tile

Inspiration ↗

After

Skip ahead to page 262 to see mood boards for the rest of the house!

Jazzy's FAVORITE PLACES TO SHOP FOR BATHROOM ACCESSORIES

Anthropologie	The Little Market
CB2	Olive & Linen
Etsy	Society6
The Garage Collective	Target
Leif	World Market

Jazzy's CHAPTER 6 CHECKLIST

☐ Did you complete the Everything Bathroom Checklist on page 269 so you know what you need for your bathroom project?

☐ Did you double-check that your tile selections won't hurt the resale value of your house?

☐ Did you pick really fun lighting, wallpaper, and bathroom accessories to put your house-story stamp undoubtedly on your bathroom?

If you answered "no" to any of the above, you have more work to do!

7 FIREPLACES, BOOKCASES, AND HIDDEN SPACES

"These are places in your home that are begging to showcase your personal style and maybe even make your life a bit easier."

When you were a kid, did you wish you had a bookcase that opened up to a secret room when a specific book was pulled? I know I did! Well, guess what? We can have that as adults! That's right. This chapter is all about making the most of your house and adding those spaces that will make your life more functional, less cluttered, prettier, and a whole lot more fun.

On my TV show, two of the things I'm known for are transforming dated fireplaces into beautiful focal points and upgrading a home's functionality with super cool, how-did-you-even-think-of-that features. Sometimes these features are hidden spice racks for home chefs, secret dog caves for our favorite furry friends, or disguised TVs in unique places. Sometimes the functional breakthrough is a really great built-in bookcase that turns clutter into cuter (see what I did there?). Other times it's as simple as adding some book ledges and some pretty baskets. The point is there's a way to hide or organize something to take your space to the next level, and I bet you haven't even thought of it yet. Don't worry, I have some ideas.

Let's look at our fireplaces, our empty walls, and our clutter piles with a whole new perspective. These are places in your home that are *begging* to showcase your personal style and maybe even make your life a bit easier. We'll go ahead and start with the fireplace . . . not sure a fireplace can make your life easier, but I promise you that we can make it WAY cooler.

Fireplaces

We all know of a fireplace that we wish was something of great architectural interest but is actually just blah, boring, bland, and right *smack dab* in the middle of the room. I've even seen my clients go to great lengths to hide their ugly fireplaces. Guys, when I said, "hidden spaces," I didn't mean to hide the fireplace. But hey, we don't need to go there—we can make it better! Let's chat about all the ways you can make your fireplace the beautiful, functional, focal point of the room. Okay, but where to start with your fireplace? You guessed it! The fireplace needs to fit within your house story from chapter 1. So, whether you're building a brand-new house and picking everything from the firebox to the tile to the mantle or you're trying to buy a new fireplace screen for your rental fireplace—you start at the same place.

The Three Easiest Ways to Update Your Fireplace

Accessories: Fireplace screens, fire sets, a cute basket of logs—you can drastically change the look of your fireplace for very little money. Maybe a few well-considered accessories are all you need!

Paint: I've painted a *lot* of brick fireplaces in my day. I've also whitewashed, lime-washed, dyed, micro-cemented, plastered . . . you name it, I've tried it. If you're willing to part with your red brick fireplace, GO FOR IT! Just know that these are permanent changes, so look at lots of photos online, read all the tutorials, and double-check that what you're doing is part of your overall house-story goal.

Mantle: Honestly, adding a mantle is not that hard! I'm sure you've seen me on TV with my carpenters installing these beautiful giant beams above gleaming new fireboxes and thought, "Yeah, right, like it's that easy." Well . . . it is! You can go to your local lumber yard and find a nice big piece of wood (measure your firebox and the wall you intend to install on before venturing out), then bring it home, clean it up, and mount it on your wall. Again, online tutorials are your friends, and if you really don't want to tackle this yourself, this is an inexpensive thing to pay a carpenter to do—but it will make a huge impact!

Texture

My favorite fireplaces usually have a few different textures to them. I won't say it's a "rule," but when I use two or three textures in my design, that's when my fireplaces look the best. So, for example, in the following image we kept the brick (texture 1) but painted it, then we added a vintage wooden beam for the mantle (texture 2), and added simple, smooth drywall (texture 3) on the rest of the wall. Any of these textures by themselves = BORING. But when you put them all together, they work to create something interesting!

Pro Tip: Call a local fireplace store or barbecue distributor, and for very little money they can install a "log set" that will make your gas fireplace feel brand new. Most of them even have a battery-operated remote so you can start your fire with the touch of a button. Talk about setting the mood!

Texture 3

Texture 2

Texture 1

Bookcases   I'm sure we all have that really beautiful, not real-life "how do they do it?" home account we follow on social media. They always seem to have everything just right, and their shelves are never boring or cluttered. How *do* they do it? Well, first of all, it's social media, folks, not real life. But second of all, they've probably mastered the art of storage. Storage is one of those things that is *tough*. Just when you think you have it all figured out, your kids grow up or your interests or hobbies change, and suddenly you have to rethink everything. Don't despair and definitely don't underestimate the value that great, functional storage solutions can bring to your life. I love taking a big wall or corner of *nothing* and turning it into *something*. Whether that's adding a built-in bookcase or some sort of shelving system, finding ways to organize stuff in a beautiful display is never a bad move.

If you can figure out how to simply add a single basket, or hook, or little shelf that wasn't there before—I think that's a win! So, let's chat about all the ways you might be able to add a little bit more organization (and maybe a little fun) into your life—because, after all, you need stuff to post online, too, right? #shelfie

First Things First

Let's make a moment out of nothing. The first step to figuring out if a bookcase (or a "built-in," as we call it in the biz) is right for your home is deciding if you have the space for it. Usually a blank wall (or even better, a nook or alcove) is your best friend when it comes to adding storage. There are certain cases when a great piece of art is the perfect thing for a blank wall. But before you jump to the conclusion to hang art on a wall because it's a blank wall, think about the functionality of it and whether there's a better way to use that wall. In some cases, a built-in is exactly what your space or formerly blank wall needs. If you open up the possibility for it, this could be so much more than a blank wall. Maybe it's been waiting all this time to help you declutter the rest of the house, add some great visual interest to your space, and—even better— MAKE YOU HAPPY! So, yeah, adding a built-in is basically like therapy—I said it.

Once you identify the location where you think a built-in might work, the next step is to find some inspiration. I love following designers online; I use website Houzz.com all the time, and I'm borderline religious when it comes to Pinterest. Find a few photos that make your heart beat a little faster and share them with your contractor or carpenter. If you're really ambitious, you can try this yourself. There are lots of cute ways to use floating shelves from Pottery Barn, West Elm, and CB2 to create the look of a built-in for a fraction of the price. If you're feeling crafty, go for it! Otherwise, call in the pros; it's totally up to you.

Shop Your Home

Now you have the bookcase or built-in of your dreams, but you're stuck— what do you put on all those pretty shelves? My advice: Don't buy ANYTHING! That's right, chances are there are items in your house that will look great on the shelves while telling a story or adding functionality. I always ask clients, "What have you brought home from a trip or have from your graduation, your wedding, or the birth of your child that makes you smile every time you see it but is tucked away in a drawer or closet?" Those things are what should be going on these shelves. Maybe you buy a few shadow boxes to display memorabilia (think old ticket stubs, playbills, or even speeding tickets), maybe you brought some shells home from a beach vacation that you can put in a mason jar, or maybe you have books that are scattered around your house that you can collect into a few stacks. Whatever you decide to put on these shelves, if it's yours and it's special, it will make you that much happier.

INSIDER SECRETS

Do you ever see a home on an HGTV show and wonder why all the books in the design are turned around backward? It's not because it's a cool trend (though, this look has become super popular in recent years)—it's because the titles are trademarked. If the spines were facing out, the TV network would have to get permission to show each title. So, instead, the books are turned spine-in for filming! Feel free to share that juicy detail at your next cocktail party or BBQ.

Rules of Styling Built-Ins

Put at least one (if not three) plants on the shelves of your built-ins. This might come as a surprise, but I use faux plants on my shelves all the time. Why? Because they don't die! But honestly, faux plants have come so far from the fake ivy of our youth—I've even accidentally watered a faux cactus in my own house. Whoops! So stock up on a few faux plants and put them on the shelf first.

Gather items in groups of three. This is a tried-and-true styling rule because it works! Instead of putting two items next to each other that will compete for symmetry, try to gather your items into sets of three. This will allow for more visual interest and be pleasing to the eye.

Layer, layer, layer! Taller things in the back, shorter things in the front. Don't be scared to stack books and then put an object on top of the stack. Mix and match textures and add in a few unexpected items to get the conversation started!

Jazzy's FAVORITE PLACES TO SHOP FOR FAUX PLANTS

Crate & Barrel	Pottery Barn
IKEA	Target

TALKING TO THE PROS

I get it: talking to a carpenter about plans for your house can feel a little intimidating, to say the least! When you combine construction lingo you don't understand with the pressure to effectively communicate exactly what you want in your home, you get a whole bundle of nerves. My carpenter is basically my best friend now because of all the projects we've done together, and even I sometimes have trouble communicating my plans. Here are the four tips I use to make sure we're speaking the same language.

1. Find lots of inspiration photos that show what you'd like replicated in your own home. If possible, text or email the photos to your carpenter ahead of your meeting.

2. Type up any notes or questions you may have and print them out for yourself and your carpenter. That way when you meet, you can refer to them and take additional notes on them if needed. You won't have to worry about remembering to ask something because you'll have it right in front of you!

3. During the meeting, don't be afraid to question what the carpenter says or bring up any ideas that you have. No question is a dumb question, and sometimes asking more questions is a key part of the creative process. Say what you think, and don't feel like you're going to offend the carpenter. Push back if you need to, and if you have an idea, say it. They aren't mind readers—and if they can successfully create what you're hoping for, everybody's going to be happier in the end.

4. At the end of your meeting, recap the plan or type up what was discussed in the meeting and send it to your carpenter in a follow-up email.

Hidden Spaces

Clients always ask me, "How did you ever think to install that secret bar in your client's house on TV?" Or "How did you know to put a dog cave under the stairs?" And my answer is always the same: "Well, don't you think it's cool?" Basically, what I'm getting at is you already know if something sounds like a cool idea, you just have to GO FOR IT! If you're like me, you've always dreamed of having a secret bookcase in your house. Or a secret passageway to a secret room . . . you get the picture. Also, I bet you jammed yourself into closets, cabinets, and homemade forts when you were a kid, too, right? We all have this "fun gene"; we just have to stop being boring adults and let our fun flag fly! Not all of us will get the secret room of our dreams, but that doesn't mean we won't keep trying.

Secret Storage

A secret room bonus? While being cool is its obvious perk, secret spaces can act as secret storage to keep stuff tucked away until it's ready to be used. And it's not just secret rooms that can help us hide our crap. It's actually just that boring old S-word: storage. So, if you're too scared to add a secret room, don't for a second be too scared to add storage. We've all gotten the call—"Guess what? I'm in town and I'll be over in five minutes." Cut to the cartoonlike scene where we jam everything on the floor into an overflowing closet, using our legs like extra arms to pick up laundry, toys, dog beds, and throw pillows. Our guest arrives, and we're a little sweaty and just pray that the closet door doesn't pop open. We can avoid this scenario! Look around your house and you might realize you're using only a fraction of the space. I don't mean you're only "filling" a fraction of the space, but actually *using*—there's no way you're maxed out! Something I do regularly for my clients is help them focus on storage solutions that will actually work for them. Find a coffee table that stores your blankets, get some big baskets to hold your toys, and please, please, please get something to put your shoes in by the front door.

THE KIDS ARE TAKING OVER

Your kids are the light of your life, but, man, their toys seem to be EVERYWHERE. We can share our spaces with our kids without our living rooms feeling like a toy store—I promise, it's possible! Take a few easy steps to designate organized toy storage so your home's common areas stay clutter-free.

Hang some book ledges. You know those long and shallow shelves with a lip on the front edge and a groove notched in for books? They're a great way to corral books and have them easily accessible. Hang the shelves low enough so the kids can reach for the books on their own. Plus, this becomes functional art—win-win!

Grab some hot wheels. No, I'm not talking about the toy cars. Shop for baskets with wheels or large canvas bins with wheels on the bottom. These are great for toy storage so you don't have to carry them and hurt your back—you can just roll them where they need to go. It may even make cleanup more fun for the kiddos (and more successful)!

Hide toys in plain sight. Baskets or cubed bins are a great way to have toys hidden in plain sight while making them part of your decor. Work baskets into your built-in or buy a piece of furniture that has a place to tuck in some baskets or bins. You can store toys that can be easily pulled out at playtime and slide them right back into their storage spot when they're not in use. Store like items together (LEGOS with LEGOS, art supplies with art supplies, games with games . . . get it?) to keep everything organized and easy to find.

Behold: The Power of Baskets

Just like how we talked about hiding toys in plain sight with baskets, this applies for all your other stuff too. The main thing that I see my clients doing wrong when it comes to using baskets is buying baskets that are too small. Although a bigger basket can cost a bit more money, having a basket that can actually fit or effectively corral your stuff can make all the difference. The way I approach buying baskets is I take everything out of the closets, cabinets, boxes (if you're moving), and I put them into piles on the floor. This is called the "It's gonna get worse before it gets better" phase. Once you have made your piles, then you can determine what would fit well in a basket together and what size your basket should be. For example, let's say you make a pile of blankets in the living room. Instead of jamming the blankets into a cabinet, you might realize you have enough blankets to fill a smart-looking basket instead. This now leaves your cabinet open for other, less pretty things.

And don't forget, baskets—like any decor you choose—can add to or detract from your house story. So, make sure you pick ones that speak to you but would feel cohesive in your space at the same time. Most baskets are pretty neutral, so, chances are, if you find a basket you like, it will go nicely with the rest of your decor.

OTHER THINGS I LIKE TO PUT IN BASKETS:

Backpacks	Shoes
Beach towels	Sports equipment
Pet gear	Umbrellas

Jazzy's FAVORITE PLACES TO SHOP FOR BASKETS

Jungalow	Vintage and flea markets
Target	West Elm
Urban Outfitters	World Market

Make It Personal

Make your storage work for you! Maximize your space and really *use* it! Let's look at your nooks and crannies with fresh eyes. There's a world of possibility hiding in your house, you just have to find it.

ARE YOU A BOOKWORM?

ARE YOU A COFFEE LOVER?

ARE YOU A PET LOVER?

ARE YOU A HOME COOK?

ARE YOU AN AVID TV WATCHER?

Be Practical

Now that you've seen the secret world of hidden-space possibilities, it's easy to get carried away. I love the enthusiasm, and I'm not telling you to pump the brakes on the creativity, but I *do* want you to be practical with your ideas. I don't advise putting a hidden door on anything you need to find on a daily basis or that you use every day. It's never going to be as functional as a regular door, and the novelty is going to wear off quickly when you try to go into your pantry for the fifth time that day. Or let's say your cool hidden door isn't so cool anymore when Grandma can't find the coat closet the entire time she's staying at your house. Use a hidden door for something that's fun and extra, like a kids' fort or a wine room or a little speakeasy or a movie room—you get the picture!

Jazzy's CHAPTER 7 CHECKLIST

☐ Have you come up with a way to display something in your house that needs showing off?

☐ Will you "let your fun flag fly" and not be too "adult-y" while looking for innovative storage solutions?

☐ Did you buy a basket? No, really—go buy a basket!

If you answered "no" to any of the above, you have more work to do!

8

PERSONALIZE AND DIYS—TELLING YOUR HOUSE STORY

"Someone who has never met you should be able to walk into your house and immediately know who you are and what you're about."

It's the last chapter and it's time to get funky! Have you ever wanted a playful indoor swing in your living room or a rope wall that breaks up your open-concept entryway? What about customized wallpaper, a place to display your vintage lunch-box collection, or even just a fun way to frame your family selfies? Because let's be honest, all these things are part of your life, and they make you happy! The key to making your home feel undeniably you is putting your passions, hobbies, family, history, and memories on display and treating them like art.

You know how on TV, when a family walks into the house I've just completed for them, the happy tears start to flow? Well, you can have that same feeling in your own house. If you can be true to yourself and incorporate into your home the quirky and fun things that make you special, your home will tell the story of YOU, and that's really what matters at the end of the day. Where to start? Here are a few ideas.

Think About Your Favorite Hobby

Do you have a vintage record collection? Does your family karaoke on the regular and have dance parties that rock the neighborhood? Maybe a family music corner or record room is right for you!

Are you known in your friend group as the ultimate book-club, game-day, or wine-tasting host? Having a super-stocked wine setup, a place for people to gather, or an outdoor TV lounge would really take your get-togethers to the next level.

Or perhaps you're a globetrotter and you can't wait to head off on your next adventure, bringing treasures home along the way. A cool curio cabinet would be a perfect place to showcase your far-off finds, or maybe you can create a photo wall with all of your destination shots.

Whatever your thing might be, if you have a way to incorporate a hobby or favorite pastime into your house, it will always feel like home. And while a perfectly styled home we see online, in magazines, or on TV will always be the best #inspo jumping-off point for ideas, the most beautiful homes are ones that tell the stories of the unique people who live inside them. So, think about what makes you YOU—what makes you feel happy, inspired, safe, connected, comfortable—and translate that into your decor. After all, the best reaction is someone stepping into your home for the first time, grinning, and exclaiming, "Wow, this is so *you*!"

THE HOST

THE TRAVELER

THE WINE LOVER

THE SURFER

Think About What Makes You Comfy

Does your living room feel like the spot to be after a long day, where you can kick up your feet and relax? If not, what's missing? Let's identify your needs based on your daily routine, lifestyle, and personality to curate a space that's truly customized to you and your family.

If you spend a lot of time at home, make sure your space functions properly for that. Ensuring everything has a place will keep your stress levels down and make your living room ready to welcome you at all times. If you have kids, this might mean some pretty as well as clever storage solutions (flip back to chapter 7). If you work from home and use the living room, make sure you have a place to stow your work materials at the end of the day so you can truly unwind. If you have family and friends over often, equip your living room with plenty of seating. And most important, do what works best for you and your family. It can be easy to think, "Well, a couch isn't supposed to face this way" or "Should I put a TV in front of the window?" but when all is said and done, this is your home. It's most important that it functions well for the people who spend all their time there (including you!).

Ways to Make Your Living Room Cozy

Being cozy is not just about having a soft blanket (although that helps)—it's also about being comfortable in your space. It's about your space being livable. We've all seen places on social media that make you feel like you live in a shack in comparison, and maybe make you think your house could never look that way, but it *can*. You just have to figure out how to use what you already have, maybe add a few new items, and if your living room makes you happy, it will also feel like that photo you see on social media or in a design magazine.

Steps:

Layer rugs.

Add a plant.

Add something vintage.

Add personal photos.

Stack some books.

Install a dimmer on your lights or add task lighting.

Don't Ignore History

We all have something from our past (maybe from 100 years ago or maybe from last week) that has a fun story associated with it. Or maybe you've inherited some really great mementos from family members or friends. I challenge you to take these pieces of history and incorporate them into your home's design. They'll help tell your house story while adding that must-have layer of "something vintage" that's so important to a well-rounded room. Every room needs something with a little patina on it—trust me.

Cover Your Walls with Cool Stuff

We've all heard it: art is subjective. Well, it's true! What I like, you might not like, and you know what? That's okay! Following are some ideas of where to start when it comes to filling up your blank walls and getting an extra dose of personal style in your house.

Frame a Saying

What's your favorite saying? Wouldn't you want to see it on the wall every day? A great way to make art is to use the things you say every day as inspiration. Maybe you have a family mantra or a motto that means a lot to you. Seeing those words every day would surely bring a smile to your face each morning or get you through a tough day. Think outside the box on this one—I'm talkin' song lyrics, mottos, wedding vows, words printed on flags . . . you get the idea. And a word of advice: From someone who *loves* to use words in their designs, try not to overdo it. Make sure the sayings you display are personal and meaningful to your family, otherwise the words might come off as clichéd.

I JUST CALLED
TO SAY
I LOVE YOU

Take it easy

GIVE A
DAMN

Custom Wallpaper

Did you know that photos can be made into wallpaper? No, really—there are some great companies out there that specialize in creating custom wallpaper. Sometimes a giant photo mural of you standing on a mountain is just what your space might be missing!

Not into photo wallpaper? That's fine! Maybe you're more into a zippy wallpaper with a bold pattern. And by the way, you don't have to wallpaper a whole room for maximum impact . . . sometimes papering only one wall in a room (or even better—a little niche or nook!) is the perfect amount of POP.

Photo Memory Wall

One of my signature design moves is to make an EPIC photo wall. I've done this on TV, I've done it in family members' homes, and I've done it in my own home. It's just that good! All you have to do is hang a few picture ledges, buy a bunch of frames, and fill them with your favorite photo memories. These can be iPhone photos, people—I want to see those dog noses and kiddos and selfies! I like to buy frames in the same color family and print all my photos in black-and-white or sepia tone for a more monochromatic look, but really there aren't any rules! Okay, I lied: the only rule is to pick photos that make you smile. How hard can that be?

Fun Artwork

If you want to add some fun artwork to your space—something that really catches your eye and is *different*—but you don't know where to start, I've got you covered. A lot of the best artwork I find is from Society6, Minted, Juniper Print Shop, or thrifted. The key to knowing what to pick is really just paying attention to how a piece of art makes you feel. If something grabs you right away, chances are you'll like looking at it over and over again.

Another great way to infuse personality into your space is to buy art while you're traveling or visiting someplace close to your heart. This could be a print or a poster from a local shop where you're visiting—take it home, mat it, and put it in a nice frame, and it will feel like a really special piece of art. It will carry the spirit of the place you visited and remind you of your trip every time you see it. Plus, it's an instant icebreaker with your guests: "So, one time, I was in New York . . ."

HOW TO CHANGE YOUR CABINET HARDWARE
(*aka* THE CABINET HARDWARE SWITCHEROONIE!)

You've heard it from me, you've heard it from everyone: the easiest way to change the look of a bathroom or kitchen without doing construction (hello, renters!) is to change out the cabinet hardware. Chances are your cabinets have holes already drilled in them that are holding the old cabinet hardware. If not, you're lucky, and you can start fresh.

WHAT YOU'LL NEED

Cabinet or
drawer hardware

Screwdriver (an
electric screwdriver
makes this a breeze!)

STEP 1

Look at your existing cabinet and determine where the holes are drilled. Are there single knob pulls or handle pulls that have two holes? If there are two holes, measure the distance between them.

STEP 2

Go on a cabinet hardware hunt! If your cabinets have single holes, you're looking for knobs. Any knob that you like should work—a knob is a knob, so if you find a new knob you like, it should work where your old one was, no problem. If you're looking for handles, it's a little bit trickier because you have to make sure the spread of the hardware is the same width. So, for example, if your existing handles have holes that are 4 inches apart, you need to find new handles that are made to fit holes that are 4 inches apart. But don't despair—there are lots of options! You're bound to find something you like that fits your house story.

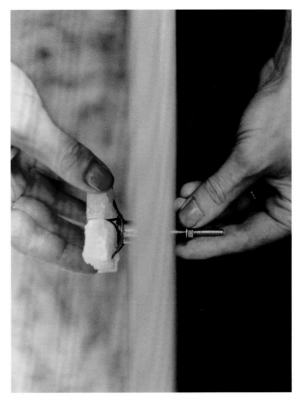

STEP 3

Once your new hardware is in hand, it's time for the switcheroonie. Take a screwdriver and unscrew the back side of the existing cabinet hardware. It should come out pretty easily. If you're a renter, you might want to save this hardware in a zip-seal bag so you can put the existing hardware back on the cabinets when you move out. Now, take your new hardware, insert the screw into the back side of the cabinet to make a knob (or handle)/cabinet/screw sandwich. Tighten the screw and you're done.

CONTINUED

LOOK WHAT I DID!

STEP 4

Make sure you take an "after" photo and share it on social media
so all your friends and family can see how handy you are.

HOW TO MAKE A DIY ROPE WALL

While open-concept floor plans can be lovely, sometimes it's nice to figure out ways to differentiate rooms or areas within an open-concept space. This DIY rope wall is a special feature I've used multiple times in many different types of homes to add a bit of structure to a more open space, while still keeping that open-concept vibe going. Maybe you want to have your living room feel like one room and your dining room feel like another, but you don't want to put up a solid wall. This rope wall is a great way to make these spaces feel like two separate rooms while still allowing you to have a line of sight and talk to people who are in the other room, all while adding style at the same time.

When choosing where to place your rope wall, make sure you plan to install this in a space that's open from ceiling to floor, as this connects to the ceiling and hangs all the way to the floor.

Wood Pro Tip: You can have any length of wood cut at your local hardware store—all you have to do is ask! This will save you from having to cut it yourself at home. See, it does make sense to measure before you go shopping.

Measuring Pro Tip: Before you shop for rope, make sure you get your measurements right. For example, let's say your future rope wall space is 4 feet wide and your ceiling is 8 feet tall. Your rope will be 2.5 inches apart from the next piece and so on. If you take 4 feet (that's 48 inches) and divide it by 2.5 inches, that means you'll need approximately 19 pieces of rope. Each piece of rope will be 9 feet long because you have 8-foot ceilings and you're adding one extra foot for knot tying. So, take 19 multiplied by 9 and you need 172 feet of rope.

CONTINUED

WHAT YOU'LL NEED

Two pieces of 1-by-2-inch wood cut to the width of rope wall you'll be creating (see Wood Pro Tip)

Can of spray paint (to match your ceiling)

Electric drill and (drillbit slightly wider than your rope)

Sharp scissors

Natural manila rope, 0.5-inch diameter (see Measuring Pro Tip)

Tape (preferably something sturdy yet pliable, like painter's tape)

Two or three ceiling hooks

Two or three eye hooks

STEP 1

Lay the wood pieces down on a drop cloth or large piece of cardboard and spray-paint the wood. Make sure you shake that can well! Hold the can of spray paint about 6 inches away from your wood piece and spray it in even motions to get a consistent coat. Once the sides you painted have dried, flip your wood pieces over and spray the other sides. Make sure all sides of the wood pieces are coated evenly in the paint. Leave them to dry.

STEP 2

Once the paint has dried, prop your wood on something like two sawhorses or two overturned buckets. Drill holes into the pieces about 2.5 inches apart, in the middle of the wood on the wide side, drilling the same number of holes as pieces of rope you need to make your wall. Make sure you match your holes on each wood piece so that they'll line up, from top to bottom, when a rope is threaded into each hole.

STEP 3

Prepare your rope. Measure your rope and make the appropriate cuts based on your measurements for the wall space you're creating and your ceiling height. Don't forget to add that extra foot of length for tying knots! Once you note each measurement, cover the rope segment you're about to cut with the tape. Cut in the middle of the tape and through the rope—this trick prevents your rope from fraying. Keep the tape on your rope ends until you've finished threading and knotting the rope pieces.

CONTINUED

STEP 4

Thread your taped rope ends through the holes
you drilled into the wood pieces and tie knots
at the end of each rope length. Do this on both
wood pieces from end to end so your order looks
like this: knot, wood piece, length of rope, wood
piece, knot. Remove the tape when you've finished
knotting the rope ends.

STEP 5

Screw your ceiling hooks into the ceiling, spreading
them out in a line where you intend to hang your
rope wall (it might help to tape a line on your ceiling
where you intend to hang your rope wall so you
can screw in your hooks in a straight line). Measure
your hook placements and echo those on the wood
piece that will serve as the top piece, marking with
tape (or a pencil) so you don't lose your place. Screw
your eye hooks into those places.

STEP 6

Once you've screwed in both your ceiling hooks and eye hooks, it's time to hang your rope wall! Carefully gather the top wood piece (the one with the eye hooks) and hook it onto the corresponding ceiling hooks. Ta-da! You have a wall now, and bonus: you can remove it whenever you want.

HOW TO MAKE A DIY CUSTOM HOUSE NUMBERS SIGN

There's a photo from one of my *Hidden Potential* projects that's continued to be extremely popular on Pinterest and Instagram. No matter how many times this project is posted and reposted, people love it and can't seem to get enough of it! What's baffling (and kind of funny) to me is that it's just a photo of someone's house numbers! For years, fans have asked me on social media, "Where'd you get that sign house number? Where can I buy them?" And I always laugh to myself because I made it! They can't be bought anywhere—but I can tell you how to make one yourself.

First off, some backstory. It was the day before a big reveal—which is when we show the homeowners how we fixed up their house. There are usually some tears and some OMGs. Anyway, I was driving home from this project—the California Cape Cod from season 1, episode 12—and I was thinking this home just needed *one more* cool custom touch. I stopped at Home Depot and picked up some simple, modern house numbers; they probably cost me no more than $50. Once I got home, I grabbed a piece of plywood from my scrap wood pile and got to work. I stayed up late that night putting this together, and the next morning when I handed over the keys to the homeowners, there was a one-of-a-kind set of house numbers on the front of their house. This project is seriously so easy . . . the only thing that takes a few hours is waiting for the primer to dry.

WHAT YOU'LL NEED

A piece of plywood
(make sure it fits
your numbers)

Simple, modern
house numbers

Sanding block or
sandpaper

A paint brush

KILZ primer

A paper plate

Wood stain

An old rag

A drill or rubber
mallet (optional)

Jazzy's FAVORITE PLACES TO SHOP FOR HOUSE NUMBERS

Design Within Reach

Hardware stores

Modern House Numbers

Rejuvenation

West Elm

STEP 2

Lightly sand the wood to make the edges and corners less sharp.

STEP 1

You can take your wood with you to the hardware store to buy house numbers or take your house numbers to your lumberyard—whichever comes first, make sure you use one to inform the other so everything fits. If you need your wood cut to fit your numbers, you can ask your hardware store to help you with that.

STEP 3

Dip the paint brush in some KILZ primer and dab it on the paper plate before applying to the wood. This should be thick, but it doesn't need to cover all the wood. Let dry.

CONTINUED

STEP 4

Once your primer has dried, apply wood stain with a rag over the entire wood board. The exposed wood parts without primer will soak up the stain, and the primed parts will get darker and "dirtier" looking. Wipe off the excess stain. Let dry.

STEP 5

Install your house numbers onto the plywood per the manufacturer's instructions. (I needed to use a drill and a rubber mallet.)

STEP 6

Hang your new plywood house number sign on your house. Enjoy!

HOW TO LAYER RUGS

One of the main questions I'm asked on social media and my blog is how to actually layer rugs. The concept is pretty simple: you take one rug and lay it on top of another. But the execution can be a little tricky. If you follow my work closely or if you've watched my show a time or two, you might have noticed this design move of mine. If you're like, "Huh? Why use two rugs when you only need one to cover a space?" let me lay(er) it on you. There are two reasons to layer rugs.

> **REASON NO. 1:** This is a really good way to bring on the texture! If you have a room that feels kind of cold or stark, layering rugs is a great step toward making it feel warm and multidimensional in its design. Not to mention, it makes for a refreshing design statement. Can't hate that!

> **REASON NO. 2:** Layering rugs is an effective way to get the look you want and stay in your budget at the same time. For example, let's say you need an 8-by-10-foot rug for your space, and you have your heart set on a kilim rug, but you can't afford that kilim price for such a large rug. Buy an inexpensive jute or natural fiber rug in your 8-by-10-foot size (Amazon always has great options at good prices!). Then buy the kilim rug or other patterned rug at the size you can afford. Layer the pretty patterned rug on top of the natural fiber rug. The natural fiber rug's job is to ground the space in the correct scale for your room, and the patterned rug sets the style and color theme for your space. If you were to use only the patterned rug in the size you can afford, it might look dinky and off in your space because it wouldn't be the right size. In the future, when the time comes that you want to change up your look, just swap out the top rug!

CONTINUED

HUNTINGTON BEACH
CALIFORNIA

A FEW TIPS TO KEEP IN MIND

Your bottom rug should fit your space properly. Take out a roll of tape and tape off where the rug would go in your room, considering that the furniture in the room should have at least one leg on the rug. So, if you're layering rugs in your living room, first measure your space and your couch.

You want your rug to sit under the couch and be out of the walkway in a small room. If the room is huge and feels really open, you can buy a rug that's large enough to cover the walkway and have all furniture in the room with at least two legs on the rug.

The top layered rug can either center on the bottom rug in a smaller area or define a section of a larger space. For example, my daughter's nursery is a relatively large room, but I wanted it to feel cozy, so I blanketed the entire room in one giant rug. Her nursery has a sitting area that I wanted to delineate as its own space separate from the crib area, so I layered a rug on that side of the room. A couch and coffee table sit on that layered rug, making it feel like its own little room within a room. On the other side of the room, the crib sits only on the large bottom rug layer. If you're using a smaller layered pairing, I'd recommend that the top rug stays within 1 to 2 feet of the bottom rug measurements. So, if your bottom rug is 8 by 10 feet, your top rug should be a 5-by-8-foot size.

Consider texture, pattern, and color when choosing your pairing. If you choose to layer two rugs that are the same color or texture, the combination may not read the way you want it to. I always find that the best impact is achieved when there's some contrast between the two rugs. Just make sure they aren't too similar, and you'll do great!

Jazzy's CHAPTER 8 CHECKLIST

☐ Is your home somewhere you really want to hang out, spend time, have your friends and family over—are you proud of your home?

☐ Is your house story front and center in your home, inside and out, for *sure*?

☐ Do you feel confident to take on updates to your home, whether it's buying a basket for toys or chatting up a contractor about a brand-new project? Are you ready?

If you answered "no" to any of the above, you have more work to do! But that's okay; this stuff can take time. I encourage you to use this book as a companion as you tackle each part of your house. Go back to the corresponding chapters for each project you take on in your home and read them again. I promise you the answers are there!

If you answered "yes" to all of the above: YAY! Seriously, I'm so proud of you! Thanks for hanging with me and listening to all my advice—hopefully now your home tells your very own house story.

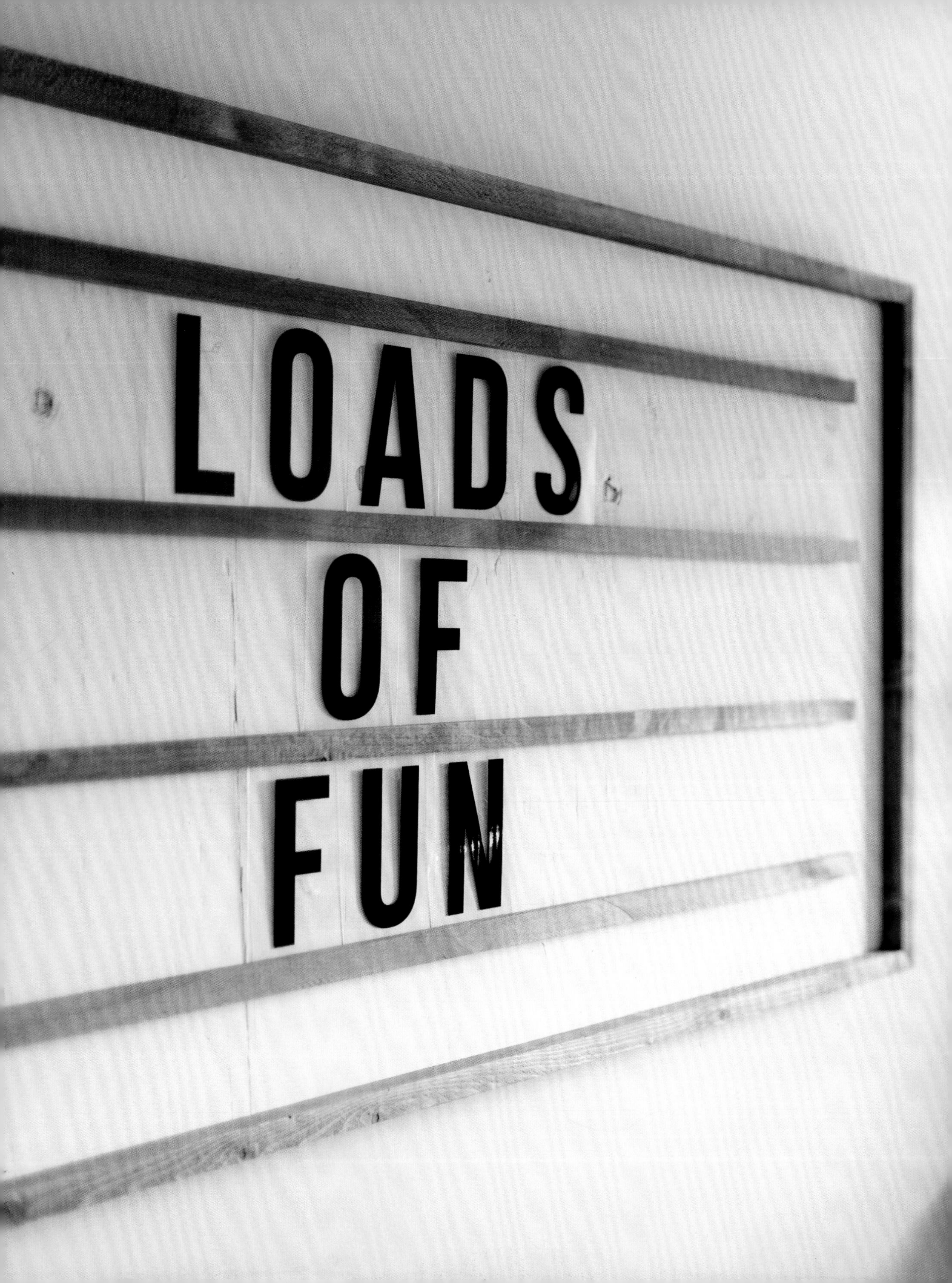
LOADS
OF
FUN

THE
ULTIMATE JAZZY'S PICKS
Three Home Designs

Like a menu plan found in the back of a cookbook, these are my hand-selected picks for three of the core styles that I introduced—you're welcome! This is a shortcut helper tool for anyone who just wants to know exactly what details I'd personally pick to design a home. So, you can take these mood boards on pages 14, 16, and 19; get the same or similar products, paint colors, and materials; and then just plug and play with your own home.

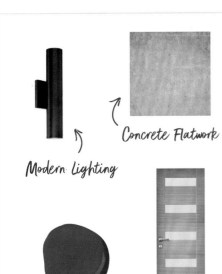

Modern Lighting

Concrete Flatwork

Stucco Color "Shoji White" by Sherwin-Williams

House Numbers →

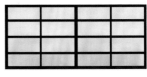

Panelled Window

Sleek Stainless Doorbell

Organic Grasses in Planters

Exterior House Paint Color "Black Fox" by Sherwin-Williams

MidMod Door

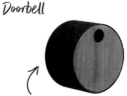

Modern Birdhouse

Satin Nickel Handleset

Industrial-Steel Awning Inspiration

Wall Sconces Over Art

Custom Barn Door

Gray Roller Shades

Smoked-Wood Floors

Simple-Shaker Style Doors

Brass Cabinet Hardware

Wall-Mounted Toilets

Interior Wall Color "Pediment" by Sherwin-Williams

Lever Door Hardware

CONTINUED

CONTEMPORARY ORGANIC MIDMODERN | KITCHEN

White Subway-Tile Backsplash

Leather Stools at Breakfast Bar

Lower Cabinets Painted "Extra White" by Sherwin-Williams

Oversize Basket Pendant Lighting

Chimney-Style Hood

Quartz Marble-Look Countertops

Pull-Down Faucet

Open Shelving with Brass Brackets

Stainless Appliances

CONTEMPORARY ORGANIC MIDMODERN | LIVING ROOM

Porcelain Tile Floors

Fireplace Inspiration

Wood Ceiling Concept

Sleek Ceiling Fan

Oversize Jute Rug

Durable Coffee Table

Cozy Pillows

Low Leather Couch

Floors in Chevron Marble Mosaic Tile

Handcrafted Modern Mirror

Wall Sconce Above Mirror

Bathroom Inspiration ↑

Shower Trim with Push-Button Diverter

Quartz Countertops

Cozy Towels for Guests →

Occasional Seating

Wall Lighting Above Nightstands

Faux Plant

Colorful Bedroom Inspiration ↑

↑ Modern Dog Bed

Simple White Bedding →

Wool Rug ↙

VINTAGE CRAFTSMAN COTTAGE | EXTERIOR

Industrial Wall Sconces

Vintage-Style Brass Doorbell

Front Door Painted "Spearmint" by Sherwin-Williams

456

Art Deco House Numbers

All Trim Painted "Pure White" by Sherwin-Williams

Front Door Light

Maintenance-Free Decking

Cheery Front Door Inspiration

Matte Black Handleset with Electronic Keypad

Flowering Tree in Front Yard

Exterior House Paint Color "Grizzle Gray" by Sherwin-Williams

---

VINTAGE CRAFTSMAN COTTAGE | BASICS

Sleek Ceiling Fan

Neutral Woven Window Shades

Custom Craftsman-Style Doors

Brass Toilet-Paper Holders

Vintage-Style Doorknobs

Inspiration

Traditional Elongated Toilets

Antique Brass Cabinet Hardware

Original Floors Refinished

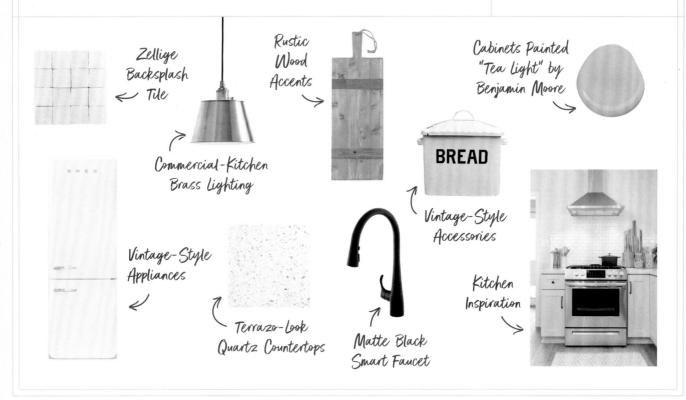

Zellige Backsplash Tile

Rustic Wood Accents

Cabinets Painted "Tea Light" by Benjamin Moore

Commercial-Kitchen Brass Lighting

BREAD

Vintage-Style Accessories

Vintage-Style Appliances

Terrazo-Look Quartz Countertops

Matte Black Smart Faucet

Kitchen Inspiration

VINTAGE CRAFTSMAN COTTAGE | LIVING ROOM

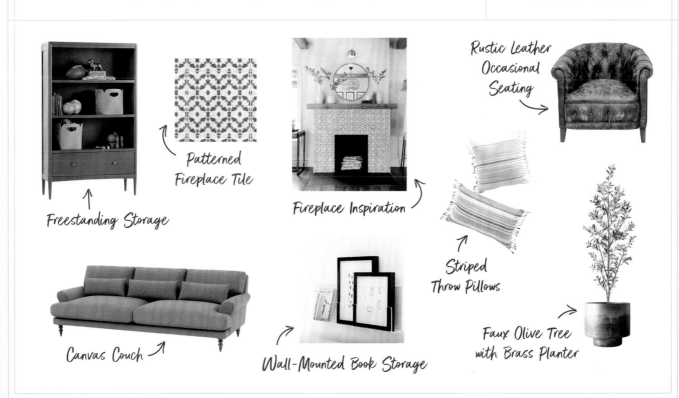

Patterned Fireplace Tile

Rustic Leather Occasional Seating

Freestanding Storage

Fireplace Inspiration

Striped Throw Pillows

Canvas Couch

Wall-Mounted Book Storage

Faux Olive Tree with Brass Planter

CONTINUED

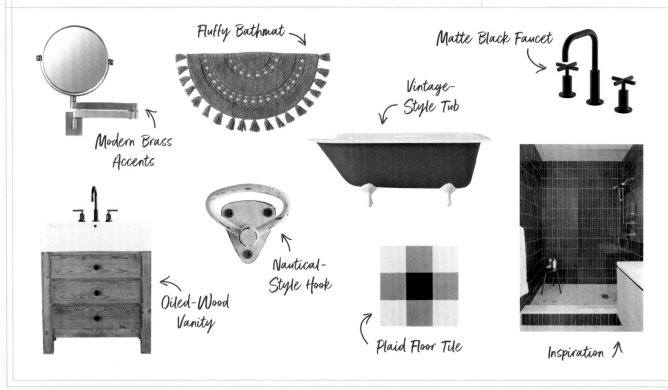

Modern Brass Accents

Fluffy Bathmat

Matte Black Faucet

Vintage-Style Tub

Nautical-Style Hook

Oiled-Wood Vanity

Plaid Floor Tile

Inspiration ↑

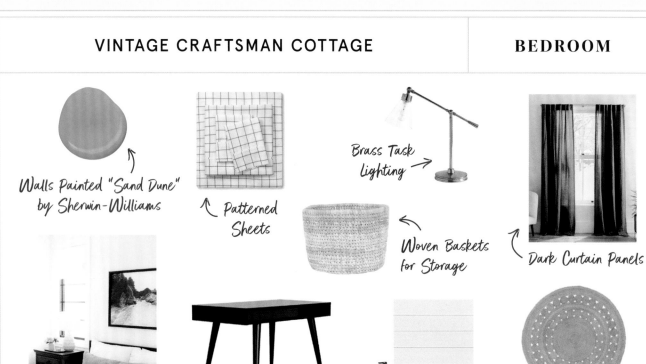

Walls Painted "Sand Dune" by Sherwin-Williams

Patterned Sheets

Brass Task Lighting

Dark Curtain Panels

Woven Baskets for Storage

Inspiration ↑

Sleek Desk

Tongue & Groove Ceiling Treatment

Round Jute Rug

TRADITIONAL INDUSTRIAL HOMESTEAD

EXTERIOR

Galvanized-Iron Wall Sconces

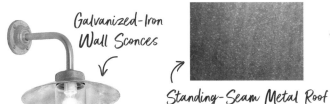

Standing-Seam Metal Roof

All Trim Painted "Frosty White" by Sherwin-Williams

Stained-Wood Front Gates

"Ring" Smart Doorbell

1 2 3

Modern Ceramic House Numbers

Exterior House Paint Color "Homestead Brown" by Sherwin-Williams

Giant Locking Mailbox

Natural Stone Bed Liners

Brown Outdoor Landscape Lighting

Front of House Concept

TRADITIONAL INDUSTRIAL HOMESTEAD

BASICS

Solid-Core White Doors

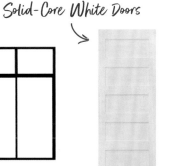

Sleek Fan

House Plant

Black Framed Windows

Simple Toilet-Paper Holders

Matte Black Door Hardware

Interior Concept

Elongated Toilets

Brushed Brass Cabinet & Drawer Pulls

Whiskey Oak Floors Upstairs

CONTINUED

TRADITIONAL INDUSTRIAL HOMESTEAD

KITCHEN

Brass Wall Sconces Above Shelves

Black Chef's Range

Nautical-Style Pendants Over Island

Cabinets in Stained Woodgrain

Shiplap Backsplash

Organic Chair

Chrome Filtered-Water Dispenser

Carrara Marble Countertops

Industrial-Style Faucet

Kitchen Concept ↑

TRADITIONAL INDUSTRIAL HOMESTEAD

LIVING ROOM

Entry Shelves Concept

Neutral Rug ↘

Rolling Ladder for Extra Storage →

Large-Format Porcelain Tile Floors

Gas Firebox

Vintage-Style Coffee Table

Textural Throw Pillows

Cozy Furniture

TRADITIONAL INDUSTRIAL HOMESTEAD | BATHROOM

Gray Flushmount Lights

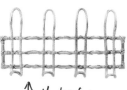
Hooks for Robes & Towels

Wallpaper Accent Wall

Rectangular Brass Mirror

Bathroom Concept

Chrome Faucets

4 Foot Wide Trough Sink

White Woodgrain Cabinets (Flanking Sink)

TRADITIONAL INDUSTRIAL HOMESTEAD | BEDROOM

Warm Hardwood Flooring

Statement Vintage-Style Pendant Lighting

Textured Storage Baskets

Midcentury Cozy Leather Seating

Traditional-Style Bedding

Bold Fabric-Look Wallpaper

Upholstered Bedframe

Plants on Nightstands

Calming Modern Art

THE
EVERYTHING KITCHEN
Checklist

This is the checklist I use on all of my kitchen projects to make sure every part of the kitchen has been considered. Use this as you plan for your own kitchen project, and nothing will fall through the cracks.

☐ Appliances (range top/oven, stove backsplash, refrigerator, freezer, microwave, dishwasher)

☐ Hood

☐ Perimeter upper cabinets (style, paint versus stain, color)

☐ Perimeter lower cabinets (style, paint versus stain, color)

☐ Island cabinet (style, paint versus stain, color)

☐ Perimeter cabinet hardware (doors versus drawers type, finish, count)

☐ Island cabinet hardware (doors versus drawers type, finish, count)

☐ Perimeter countertop (material, finish, edge detail)

☐ Island countertop (material, finish, edge detail)

☐ Backsplash (material, finish, pattern, grout color)

☐ Floor (material, finish, pattern, grout color)

☐ AV speakers and TV locations

☐ Lighting (recessed, pendants, sconces, fan)

☐ Baseboard (material, height, shape)

☐ Paint colors and sheens (base and case, door, walls, ceiling, accent walls)

☐ Windows (manufacturer, model, color, count)

☐ Doorknobs and door hinges (type, color, count)

☐ HVAC vent covers

☐ Sink(s)

☐ Faucet(s)

☐ Accessories (dish towels, soap dispenser, rugs, bar stools, pantry baskets, etc.)

☐ Other considerations (ice maker, filtered water, built-in trash, built-in recycling, built-in microwave, small appliance locker for food processor/toaster/etc., wine storage or refrigerator, USB charging plugs)

THE
EVERYTHING BATHROOM
Checklist

This is the checklist I use on all of my bathroom projects to make sure every part of the bathroom has been considered. Use this as you plan for your own bathroom project and nothing will fall through the cracks.

- ☐ Vanity cabinet (style, paint versus stain, color)
- ☐ Cabinet hardware (doors versus drawers type, finish, count)
- ☐ Countertop (material, finish, edge detail)
- ☐ Backsplash (material, finish, pattern, grout color)
- ☐ Main floor (material, finish, pattern, grout color)
- ☐ Shower floor (material, finish, pattern, grout color)
- ☐ Shower walls (material, finish, pattern, grout color)
- ☐ Shower dam (material, finish, pattern, grout color)
- ☐ Tub surround (material, finish, edge detail)
- ☐ AV speakers or TV locations
- ☐ Lighting (recessed, pendants, sconces, toilet fan)
- ☐ Baseboard (material, height, shape)
- ☐ Paint colors and sheens (base and case, door, walls, ceiling, accent walls)
- ☐ Mirror(s)
- ☐ Shower glass or shower curtain rod
- ☐ Doorknobs and door hinges (type, color, count)
- ☐ HVAC vent covers
- ☐ Toilet-paper holder
- ☐ Towel bars or towel hooks, robe hooks, hand-towel holder
- ☐ Toilet and toilet seat
- ☐ Sink(s)
- ☐ Faucet(s)
- ☐ Tub spout or filler
- ☐ Shower head (standard, rainhead, handshower, steam)
- ☐ Accessories (towels, soap dispenser, bathmats, drawer organizers, etc.)

QUICK REFERENCE TOOLBOX
Jazzy's Favorites

FAVORITE FRONT DOOR PAINT COLORS

- Benjamin Moore:
  HC 154 Hale Navy

- Benjamin Moore
  2028-30 Tequila Lime

- Sherwin-Williams:
  SW 6211 Rainwashed

- Sherwin-Williams:
  SW 7642 Pavestone

- Sherwin-Williams:
  SW 9059 Silken Peacock

- Sherwin-Williams:
  SW 6941 Nifty Turquoise

- Sherwin-Williams:
  SW 9050 Vintage Vessel

- Sherwin-Williams:
  SW 6837 Baroness

- Sherwin-Williams:
  SW 7800 Bolero

- Sherwin-Williams:
  SW 7641 Colonnade Gray

- Sherwin-Williams:
  SW 6258 Tricorn Black

- Dunn Edwards:
  DE 5390 Rubber Ducky

- Sherwin-Williams:
  SW 6509 Georgian Bay

- Sherwin-Williams:
  SW 0044 Hubbard Squash

- Sherwin-Williams:
  SW 6356 Copper Mountain

- Sherwin-Williams:
  SW 6465 Spearmint

- Sherwin-Williams:
  SW 9168 Elephant Ear

- Sherwin-Williams:
  SW 7061 Night Owl

FAVORITE INTERIOR PAINT COLORS

- Dunn Edwards:
  DEW 382 Faded Gray

- Sherwin-Williams:
  SW 7004 Snowbound

- Sherwin-Williams:
  SW 7015 Repose Gray

- Sherwin-Williams:
  SW 7631 City Loft

- Sherwin-Williams:
  SW 7008 Alabaster

- Sherwin-Williams:
  SW 7506 Loggia

- Sherwin-Williams:
  SW 7029 Agreeable Gray

- Sherwin-Williams:
  SW 7065 Argos

- Sherwin-Williams:
  SW 7641 Colonnade Gray

- Sherwin-Williams:
  SW 7005 Pure White

FAVORITE ACCENT WALL PAINT COLORS

- Benjamin Moore:
  2123-20 Caribbean Teal

- Sherwin-Williams:
  SW 6991 Black Magic

- Sherwin-Williams:
  SW 6393 Convivial Yellow

FAVORITE INTERIOR-TRIM AND CEILING PAINT COLOR

- Sherwin-Williams:
  SW 7005 Pure White

FAVORITE KITCHEN-CABINET PAINT COLORS

- Sherwin-Williams:
  SW 6465 Spearmint

- Sherwin-Williams:
  SW 7645 Thunder Gray

- Sherwin-Williams:
  SW 7749 Laurel Woods

- Sherwin-Williams:
  SW 7067 Cityscape

- Sherwin-Williams:
  SW 7005 Pure White

- Sherwin-Williams:
  SW 6258 Tricorn Black

- Sherwin-Williams:
  SW 9140 Blustery Sky

JAZZY'S FAVORITE LANDSCAPING ACCENT COLORS

Choose one of these landscaping accent colors when using my Rule of Three: Pick one accent color and two shades of green—and stick to it! Use those same three tones and plants throughout the whole project, and it will feel cohesive and look great. (See page 56 for more on choosing landscape accent colors.)

- Purple
- Orange
- White

- Yellow
- Red

FAVORITE PLACES TO SHOP FOR CABINET HARDWARE

- Anthropologie
- Build.com
- Etsy
- Rejuvenation
- Restoration Hardware
- Schoolhouse Electric
- World Market

FAVORITE PLACES TO SHOP FOR BACKSPLASH TILE

- Clé Tile
- Floor & Decor
- Hardware stores such as Home Depot or Lowe's
- Local tile showrooms
- Zia Tile

FAVORITE PLACES TO SHOP FOR FAUX PLANTS

- Crate & Barrel
- IKEA
- Pottery Barn
- Target

FAVORITE PLACES TO SHOP FOR BASKETS

- Jungalow
- Target
- Urban Outfitters
- Vintage and flea markets
- West Elm
- World Market
- Yard sales

FAVORITE BATHROOM COUNTERTOPS

- Honed Arabascato Gray porcelain by Bedrosians Tile & Stone
- Patinated copper made by a local artisan, metal worker, or metal fabricator
- Rugged Concrete quartz by Caesarstone

FAVORITE BATHROOM FAUCETS

- Kohler Purist Widespread Cross Handle, chrome
- Kohler Bridge Faucet, brass
- Kohler Single-Hole Faucet, black

FAVORITE PLACES TO SHOP FOR HARDWARE

- Baldwin
- Build.com
- Emtek
- Hardware stores such as Home Depot or Lowe's
- Rejuvenation

FAVORITE BATHROOM TILE

- Clé tile cement (floor tile)
- Thassos White marble mini-mosaic (shower pan)
- Zia Tile zellige (wall tile)

FAVORITE PLACES TO SHOP FOR MIRRORS

- Anthropologie
- CB2
- Pottery Barn
- Target
- West Elm
- Vintage markets and yard sales

RESOURCES

CHAPTER 1 **Rustic Vintage Cabin Exterior, page 21:** chair, Design Within Reach; dark stain, Benjamin Moore; firepit, Sundance Catalog; front door paint, Sherwin-Williams; inspiration photo, Rejuvenation; outdoor lighting, Seagull Lighting; pea gravel, Shutterstock; planter, Pottery Barn; post lighting, Seagull Lighting; railing, Shutterstock; stained siding, Shutterstock **Rustic Vintage Cabin Interior Details, page 21:** chair, Urban Outfitters; flag, Cotton California; grey brick, Shutterstock; kitchen inspiration, Divine Custom Homes with Bria Hammel Interiors; pendant, Etsy/Clay Café; plant, Shutterstock; sconce, Schoolhouse Electric; stove, Pottery Barn; teapot, Wayfair; toilet paper holder, Rinnai Style.

CHAPTER 4 **Flooring Types, page 100:** Brick, Armand Flooring; Carpet, Home Depot; LVP, llflooring.com; Stone, Build.com; Tile, Overstock.com; Wood, Provenza.

CHAPTER 5 **Cabinet Hardware, page 116:** Contemporary 1, Rejuvenation; Contemporary 2, Schoolhouse; Contemporary 3, House of Antique Hardware; Traditional 1, Schoolhouse; Traditional 2, Rejuvenation; Traditional 3, CB2; Rustic 1, Etsy/StichShutter; Rustic 2, Wayfair; Rustic 3, Anthropologie; Cottage 1, Anthropologie; Cottage 2, Rejuvenation; Cottage 3, Schoolhouse. **Kitchen Countertop Finishes, page 125:** Quartz, Home Depot; Granite, Bedrosians; Marble, Bedrosians; Wood, llflooring. com. **15 Fun Backsplash Ideas, page 131:** Image 1, Bedrosians; Image 2, Tile Bar; Image 3, Concrete Collaborative; Image 4, Overstock.com; Image 5, Shutterstock; Image 6, Clé Tile; Image 7, Bedrosians; Image 8, Wayfair; Image 9, Clé Tile; Image 10, Clé Tile; Image 11, Tile Bar; Image 12, Houzz; Image 13, Bedrosians; Image 14, Clé Tile; Image 15, American Tin Ceilings. **Kitchen Appliance Finishes, page 134:** Image 1, Café Appliances; Image 2, Café Appliances; Image 3, Café Appliances; image 4, Smeg USA. **Kitchen Lighting, page 140:** Contemporary 1, Design Within Reach; Contemporary 2, West Elm; Contemporary 3, Design Within Reach; Traditional 1, West Elm; Traditional 2, Shop Jasmine Roth; Traditional 3, Shop Jasmine Roth; Rustic 1, Design Within Reach; Rustic 2, Wayfair; Rustic 3, Shop Jasmine Roth; Cottage 1, Shop Jasmine Roth; Cottage 2, West Elm; Cottage 3, Shop Jasmine Roth.

CHAPTER 6 **Bathroom Tile Shapes, page 170:** Porcelain, Wayfair; Cement, Clé Tile; Wood Look, Tile Bar; Teak, Indo Teak Design; Handcrafted, Clé Tile. **Bathroom Lighting, page 180:** Contemporary 1, Rejuvenation; Contemporary 2, Shades of Light; Contemporary 3, Etsy/MODCREATION Studio; Traditional 1, Serena & Lily; Traditional 2, Rejuvenation; Traditional 3, Pottery Barn; Rustic 1, Rejuvenation; Rustic 2, Serena & Lily; Rustic 3, Pottery Barn; Cottage 1, West Elm; Cottage 2, Rejuvenation; Cottage 3, Serena & Lily. **Fave Shower Curtains, page 183:** Shower Curtain 1, World Market; Shower Curtain 2, Urban Outfitters; Shower Curtain 3, Urban Outfitters. **Fave Wallpapers, page 183:** Wallpaper 1, Anthropologie; Wallpaper 2, West Elm; Wallpaper 3, Urban Outfitters **Fave Hand Towels, page 183:** Hand towel 1, Target; Hand towel 2, World Market; Hand towel 3, Serena & Lily; Bathmat, Urban Outfitters.

APPENDIX A **Contemporary Organic Midmodern Exterior, page 259:** awning, Dan Nelson, Designs Northwest Architects; bird house, Design Within Reach; concrete flatwork, Shutterstock; doorbell, Design

Within Reach; exterior paint, Sherwin-Williams; grass, Shutterstock; handle set, Baldwin Brass Hardware; house numbers, Design Within Reach; lighting, Kichler; midmod door, Shutterstock; stucco color, Sherwin-Williams. **Contemporary Organic Midmodern Basics, page 259:** barn door, Katie Hackworth; cabinet hardware, Schoolhouse; hardware, Emtek; interior wall color, Sherwin-Williams; shades, Wayfair; Shaker-style doors, Build.com; toilet, Kohler; wall sconce, Rejuvenation; wood floors, Palladio. **Contemporary Organic Midmodern Kitchen, page 260:** 48" range, Viking; basket pendant, Shades of Light; countertops, Pentel; faucet, Grohe; hood, Viking; lower cabinets, Aristokraft.com; open shelving, Rejuvenation; stools, CB2; tile backsplash, Build.com. **Contemporary Organic Midmodern Living, page 260:** coffee table, Anthropologie; couch, CB2; fan, Lumens.com; firebox, Curbly; pillow, Shop Jasmine Roth; rug, Wayfair; tile, Tile Bar; wood ceiling, Shutterstock. **Contemporary Organic Midmodern Bathroom, page 261:** countertops, Pentel; floors, Tile Bar; inspiration photo; LL Design Co; mirror, Anthropologie; shower trim, Kohler; towels, Anthropologie; wall sconce, Schoolhouse. **Contemporary Organic Midmodern Bedroom, page 261:** chair, Anthropologie; dog bed, Crate & Barrel; inspiration photo, LL Design Co; pillows, Anthropologie; plant, Crate & Barrel; rug, Anthropologie; wall lighting, Etsy/Peared Creation. **Vintage Craftsman Cottage Exterior, page 262:** decking, Azek; door light, Rejuvenation; front door inspiration, Built Custom Homes; gray paint, Sherwin-Williams; green paint, Sherwin-Williams; house numbers, Anthropologie; toilet, Kohler; tree, Shutterstock; wall light, Rejuvenation; white paint, Sherwin-Williams. **Vintage Craftsman Cottage Basics, page 262:** toilet tissue holder, Anthropologie; fan, Bellacor; interior doors, Build.com; handle set, Home Depot; doorbell, House of Antique Hardware; flooring, llflooring.com; doorknob, Rejuvenation; living room inspiration, The Glitter Guide; shades, Wayfair; hardware, Wayfair. **Vintage Craftsman Cottage Kitchen, page 263:** breadbox, Built Custom Homes; faucet, Home Depot; tile, Livden.com; countertops, Pental; pendant light, Pottery Barn; pizza peel, Pottery Barn; cabinet paint, Sherwin-Williams; refrigerator, Smeg USA; backsplash tile, Zia Tile; kitchen inspiration, Built Custom Homes. **Vintage Craftsman Cottage Living, page 263:** pillows, Anthropologie; pot, CB2; bookshelf, Crate & Barrel; couch, Interiordefine.com; fireplace inspiration, Magnolia; plant, Nearly Natural; shelf, Pottery Barn Kids; chair, Shop Jasmine Roth. **Vintage Craftsman Cottage Bathroom, page 264:** hook, Anthropologie; floor tile, Clé Tile; inspiration photo, Emily Gilbert/Fireclay Tile; faucet, Kohler; vanity, Pottery Barn; tub, Rejuvenation; mirror, Rhmodern.com; bathmat, Urban Outfitters. **Vintage Craftsman Cottage Bedroom, page 264:** rug, Boutiquerugs.com; desk, Design Within Reach; inspiration, Juniper Print Shop; basket, Little Market; lamp, Serena & Lily; wall paint color, Sherwin-Williams; shiplap, Shutterstock; sheets, Target; curtains, West Elm. **Traditional Industrial Homestead Exterior, page 265:** doorbell, Ring.com; doorknob, Baldwin; galvanized metal, Shutterstock; house numbers, Rejuvenation; house photo of Brett & Jasmine, Built Custom Homes; mailbox, Mailboxes.com; side mount light, Lumens.com; stone, Home Depot; wall sconce, Lumens.com; windows, Shutterstock; wood sample, Signature Hardware. **Traditional Industrial Homestead Basics, page 265:** cabinet hardware, CB2; interior doors, Home Depot; fan, Kichler; toilet, Kohler; toilet tissue holder, Kohler; wood floors, Palladio; houseplant, Pottery Barn; inspiration staircase photo, *Sunset Magazine*. **Traditional Industrial Homestead Kitchen, page 266:** cabinets, Cabinet Door World; countertops, Home Depot; kitchen faucet, Luxart; kitchen concept, *Sunset Magazine*; pendant, Visual Comfort; range, Viking; shiplap backsplash, Sabbe Interiors; stool, Serena & Lily; tile floors, Eleganza; wall sconce, Original BTC; water dispenser, Insinkerator. **Traditional Industrial Homestead Living, page 266:** coffee table, Anthropologie; couch, Rove Concepts; firebox, Home Depot; ladder, First Dibs; pillow, Anthropologie; rolling ladder inspiration; The Works; rug, Burke Décor. **Traditional Industrial Homestead Bathroom, page 267:** flushmount lights, Schoolhouse Electric; hook, Shop Jasmine Roth; inspiration photo, Boston Globe Dan Curona; mirror, Restoration Hardware; trough sink, Kohler; wallpaper, Urban Outfitters; white woodgrain cabinets, IKEA. **Traditional Industrial Homestead Bedroom, page 267:** art, Juniper Print Shop; bedframe, Joss & Main; chair, Article; chrome faucets, Chicago Faucet; pendant lighting, Anthropologie; plant, Urban Outfitters; sheets, Target; storage bin, IKEA; wallpaper, Wallshoppe.

ACKNOWLEDGMENTS

To say "I never thought I'd write a book" would be a lie. This book is a giant checkmark on a lifelong bucket list, and it's also something I never could've done on my own. So I'd like to start by thanking my elementary school teachers, my camp counselors . . . just kidding. But really, we're talking about a lifetime of thank-yous I could be giving.

To Kim Perel and her fabulous team at Irene Goodman Literary Agency, thank you for believing in this book. Of all our book meetings in NYC, the one at night in the middle of a blizzard was the most memorable and a testament to your dedication. Dervla Kelly and my favorite people at Ten Speed Press and Penguin Random House—Ashley Pierce, Emma Campion, Lisa Bieser, Jane Chinn, Lauren Kretzschmar, and Andrea Portanova—I could only imagine having a dream team like you. All your creativity, insight, and unique perspectives have taken my ideas and made them reality. And, of course, my fearless agents at WME who took a chance on me and have been with me every step of the way. You keep me working, listen to my pie-in-the-sky ideas, and have helped me navigate a world I never imagined being a part of.

For making this book—Kelli Kehler as the only writer who could've stepped into my brain and patiently pulled out every little tidbit of knowledge, I can't thank you enough. Your leadership, ability to keep me on task, and friendship is appreciated more than you'll ever know. I love "mom-ing" with you! Dabito, for saying yes to this book when I stalked you so many years ago. I still stalk you; I am obsessed with your point of view and love seeing my world through your lens. Speaking of point of view, Erin Ellis, your contribution in the final hour made this book.

To my art and construction teams—where do I begin? Each project photographed is a snapshot of days, months, and—for most of us—YEARS of literal blood, sweat, and tears to make our projects come to life. For this book, Jen Chu and her "art dudes" (who includes the ever talented Miranda Ronnow) deserve the biggest shoutout and all the healthy vegan salads and sneaky mac 'n' cheese they can eat. Jen, your direction, your vision, and your ability to execute inspires me, and I respect your design opinion more than you know. To my builders and trades, there aren't enough pages in the book to list my thanks. Your ability to take my ideas and make them happen, to answer my millions of questions, to tolerate my 6 a.m. text messages on Sunday mornings that start with "So I was thinking," and especially to take the time to teach me the "how" and "why" . . . it's because of you that I have a job to go to each day. Danny and Brian, you're the A-team and it's nothing but love from the entire Roth family. Each and every photo in this book is a testament to the skill, talent, and hardworking people who brought me up in this business and have literally given me a home. I'm proud to call you my "guys" and to showcase your beautiful work in this book.

And as far as teams go, ain't none better than the one I got! To my entire Built Custom Homes team—each of you plays such a vital role in our business, in making this book, and in keeping my life on track. Kelsey and the Wildside Design team, you've stuck with me for YEARS working and reworking this book proposal, and I'm still so proud of our work. To my Shop Jasmine Roth vendors, especially the beautiful people at Creative Co-Op, thank you for your unique pieces that have woven themselves into #myjasminerothstyle. Also, Rick and Mike, your ability to capture my work for the past nine years is what started this book. You've literally been to every single project, you've captured my career, and, had it not been for COVID-19, you would've been in the delivery room when I had Hazel. Don't worry, though, I'm sure you can be there for the next one. Ha!

To HGTV and Discovery, Inc. for giving me a voice and for always having my best interest at heart. You make me look like a rock star—and for that I'm forever grateful. Your consistent support of everything I do, including this book, shows how much you care, and I can't even begin to tell you how much you've changed my life. And to all the production companies that have chosen to make TV with me for the past five years, especially my ladies at RTR Media and Lindsey Weidhorn—you found me, you groomed me, and now you have to put up with me! And to my TV crews—you're the hardest-working people I know, and you treat me like a princess. I could never live such a full life without you having my back. Your dedication and loyalty inspire me every day.

To my clients, you trusted me with your homes, you let me ask you ridiculously personal questions, and you've cheered me on at every step of my career. Thank you for being such a huge part of my story. And, of course, I can't forget my friends. You text me even when I don't respond, you like my endless social media posts, and you come to each viewing party like you've never seen me on TV before. You keep me humble, you poke fun at me, and you let me into your lives when I need it most. You remind me who I am and keep me grounded. And honestly, just knowing you have my back, is everything. #whenfriendsbecomefamily

And last, who I should have mentioned first, but they know I love them so they can be at the end of this list: my amazing family! My mom (who became a grandma while I wrote this book) for being my biggest cheerleader and the person always there to lend a helping hand. Seeing you love Hazel has given me the peace of mind to come out of maternity leave and finish this book. To Betsy for jump-starting my career through your DIY creativity, for passing on your "can do" attitude, and for letting me help you with your cottage—your grace and advice is my rock. To Ben for always wanting me to think big, for taking my work seriously, and for always encouraging Brett and me. I love that you love how much Brett and I love each other. To A & H for proofreading my proposal, for listening to every update for four years while I made this book, and for letting me completely crash your houses when it finally came time to take photos. To you and my NJ fam, thank you for cheering on my career, putting up with my wild ideas, and for keeping Brett company while I've worked like a maniac for the better part of a decade.

I'd like to dedicate this book to my best friend, husband, and forever room-mate. Brett Roth, there aren't words. You are the perfect opposite to me, yet we're the same person. And while you joke that "I don't know what Jas is up to, she just runs around," I know that you know every detail and sing my praises behind my back. Thank you for being you. I love you.

And to baby Hazel, when you can read this someday. Having my first baby (that's you!) in the middle of making this book was something I didn't expect. Your birth forever changed me, I see life completely differently, and that perspective has helped me finish this project. I see the world in your eyes and you're my whole heart. I love you, baby girl.

Making a book and being creative during such a tumultuous time in our world (hello, 2020) has given me the opportunity to persevere, to push forward, and to grow. Challenges aren't ever what we seek, but we must overcome them, find the silver lining, and appreciate the experience. This book is a reflection of all the people in my life who've supported me, believed in me, and cheered me on. This is for all of you. This book is people who love me, believe in me, and have always championed my career.

This book is every single one of you.

Published in the United States by Ten Speed Press, an imprint
of Random House, a division of Penguin Random House LLC, New York.
www.tenspeed.com

Ten Speed Press and the Ten Speed Press colophon are registered
trademarks of Penguin Random House LLC.

Library of Congress Cataloging-in-Publication Data is on file with
the publisher.

On page 21, thyme growing in pot isolated by Diana Taliun/
Shutterstock.com, black wood fence texture and background by
Sakarin Sawasdinaka/Shutterstock.com, rustic railing by Nicole
Wilcox/Upsplash, brown wall cladding on page 21 and 101 by Tim
Mossholder. Brass metal plate on page 162 by Fake Moon. On pages
14 and 259, concrete flatwork by Bhavya Kashyap/Upsplash, feather
grass by Africa Studio/Shutterstock.com, modern wooden doors
by K3Star/Shutterstock.com. Trees on page 262 by Ken StockPhoto/
Shutterstock.com. On pages 18 and 265, metal aluminum texture
by snowturtle/Shutterstock.com, large glass window by Black_Kira.
Shiplap wood texture on pages 148, 264, and 266 by Atstock
Productions/Shutterstock.com.

Hardcover ISBN: 978-1-9848-5917-4
eBook ISBN: 978-1-9848-5918-1

Printed in China

Editor: Dervla Kelly | Production editor: Ashley Pierce
Art director: Emma Campion | Designer: Lisa Schneller Bieser
Production designer: Mari Gill
Production and prepress color manager: Jane Chinn
Prop stylist: Jen Chu | Prop stylist assistant: Miranda Runnow
Copyeditor: Nancy Bailey | Proofreader: Kathy Brock
Publicist: Lauren Kretzschmar | Marketer: Andrea Portanova

10 9 8 7 6 5 4 3 2 1

First Edition